Systems Approaches to Public Sector Challenges

WORKING WITH CHANGE

D1616465

OECD

BETTER POLICIES FOR BETTER LIVES

This work is published under the responsibility of the Secretary-General of the OECD. The opinions expressed and arguments employed herein do not necessarily reflect the official views of OECD member countries.

This document and any map included herein are without prejudice to the status of or sovereignty over any territory, to the delimitation of international frontiers and boundaries and to the name of any territory, city or area.

Please cite this publication as:
OECD (2017), *Systems Approaches to Public Sector Challenges: Working with Change*, OECD Publishing, Paris.
http://dx.doi.org/10.1787/9789264279865-en

ISBN 978-92-64-27985-8 (print)
ISBN 978-92-64-27986-5 (PDF)

Photo credits: Cover © shutterstock.com/snja.

Preface

Complexity is a core feature of most policy issues today; their components are interrelated in multiple, hard-to-define ways. Yet, governments are ill equipped to deal with complex problems. Increasing automation of jobs creates new challenges for both the education and welfare systems. Ensuring a high-quality, active life for an ageing population puts pressure on the labour market, but also requires new ways of providing medical and social care. Climate change, obesity, radicalisation of social behaviours, income inequality and poverty are all challenges where causes and effects are blurred. No single public sector institution – from a solitary city to the central government – can provide adequate answers alone.

In a context of complexity and uncertainty, traditional analytical tools and problem-solving methods no longer work. Similarly, traditional approaches to public sector reform have not delivered the expected results, reflecting poor design and weak stakeholder participation, sectoral rather than whole-of-government initiatives, and inadequate evaluation.

These disappointing results have prompted government leaders across the world to ask: how do we reform differently? In particular, how do we manage increasing complexity and uncertainty? How do we deliver public services that adapt dynamically to produce viable solutions? Recognition of the "complexity gap" (the gap between the problems faced by institutions and their capacity to tackle them) has led to growing interest in systems thinking and other systems approaches such as design thinking.

A "system" in this context can be defined as elements linked together by dynamics that produce an effect, create a whole new system or influence its elements. Changing the dynamics of a well-established and complex system requires not only a new way of examining problems, but also bold decision making that fundamentally challenges public sector institutions. This entails: 1) putting desired outcomes first instead of institutional interests and resource control; 2) promoting value-based decisions (instead of simply regulating) to allow individual organisations to set their own processes to achieve shared goals; and 3) designing functions and organisations around users – not government.

Governments are struggling with adapting their policy-making approaches to account for complex system dynamics when tackling public challenges. Traditionally, public policy makers have addressed social problems through discrete interventions layered on top of one the other, building on a "cause and effect" relationship. However, these interventions may shift consequences from one part of the system to another, or simply address symptoms while ignoring causes.

Governments are at a crossroads: much of their success in dealing with complex public challenges will rely on how public systems and policies are shaped. By calling for more holistic policy approaches that look at the whole system rather than the separate parts; that value outcomes over processes; and that embrace a variety of voices and inputs instead of self-interest, systems approaches have the potential to fundamentally transform the policy-making process, allowing policy makers to focus on areas where change can have the greatest impact.

This report produced by the OECD Observatory of Public Sector Innovation (part of the Public Governance Directorate) explores how systems approaches can be used in the public sector to solve complex or "wicked" problems such as child abuse and domestic violence. Through the analysis of case studies, it describes how systems approaches can make public services more effective and resilient. The report contributes to the ongoing work of the OECD on exploring new ways of approaching public policy design and implementation, thus creating the foundations for stronger and more inclusive growth.

The report explores the theory and practice behind the use of systems approaches in tackling public challenges. The first chapter addresses the need for systems thinking in the public sector, its theoretical underpinnings and its (rare) use. The second chapter identifies a set of tactics (people and place, dwelling, connecting, framing, designing, prototyping, stewarding and evaluating) that government agencies can deploy either unilaterally or with partners to promote systems change. The third chapter provides an in-depth examination of examples of systemic change in preventing domestic violence (Iceland), protecting children (the Netherlands), regulating the sharing economy (Canada) and designing a policy framework for conducting experiments in government (Finland).

This report is an open invitation to policy makers to reflect on the systemic nature of most public sector challenges and consider how systems approaches – such as those based on integrated interventions, stakeholder engagement and reverse process engineering – can help achieve better outcomes for all.

Rolf Atler

Director for Public Governance, OECD

ACKNOWLEDGEMENTS

This report was prepared by the Observatory of Public Sector Innovation in the Public Sector Reform Division of the Governance Directorate of the OECD. The Observatory of Public Sector Innovation collects and analyses examples and shared experiences of public sector innovation to provide practical advice to countries on how to make innovation work. This project has received funding from the European Union's Horizon 2020 research and innovation programme under grant agreement No 671526.

The report has been prepared by Justin W. Cook (Senior Lead for Strategy at the Finnish Innovation Fund, SITRA and Member of Rhode Island School of Design) and Piret Tõnurist (Policy Analyst, Observatory of Public Sector Innovation, OECD) under the coordination of Marco Daglio (Senior Project Manager, Observatory of Public Sector Innovation, OECD).

The report resulted from the close cooperation with case owners, whose work was covered in the report. Special thanks to Joeri van den Steenhoven, Idil Burale, Mikko Annala, Alda Hrönn Jóhannsdóttir, Marta Kristín Hreiðarsdóttir and Marc Dinkgreve, who opened their doors to the OECD research team, and to the numerous people who participated in the interviews.

The full report benefited from comments provided by Edwin Lau, Marco Daglio, Andrea Erdei, Alex Roberts, Matt Kerlogue, Cezary Gesikowski and Jamie Berryhill. Dan Hill and Marco Steinberg help was essential in distilling key lessons from system change practice during the event. Special thanks to all the experts who sent in their comments. Marie-Claude Gohier, Liv Gaunt and Andrea Uhrhammer helped with the preparation of the final publication. Bettina Huggard and Susan Rantalainen provided administrative support.

Rolf Alter, Director of the Public Governance Directorate of the OECD and Luiz De Mello, Deputy Director have been essential in spearheading and disseminating the work in international policy making networks.

Table of contents

Executive Summary **9**

Chapter 1. **Systems approaches in the public sector: From theory to practice** **11**

Introduction 12
Managing complexity in the public sector: The case for systems approaches 14
Challenges of using systems approaches in the public sector 20
Systems approaches to public service delivery: Approaches and emerging evidence 24
Notes 32
References 34

Chapter 2. **Towards a framework for systems transformation** **41**

New systems-based practices 42
Strategies to manage complexity: What are the options for the public sector? 45
Working with relative precision 49
Toward a systems transformation process 51
Notes 63
References 65

Chapter 3. **System approaches in practice: Case studies** **69**

A systems approach to tackling domestic violence: The United Against Domestic
Violence programme (Iceland) 70
Using system approaches in policy design: introducing experimental culture as a
high-level political goal (Finland) 79
A systems approach to reshaping an organisation's purpose and working methods:
child protection services in the Netherlands 92
Using systems approaches to regulate the sharing economy: Public transportation
in Toronto (Canada) 106
Notes 118
References 120

Conclusions **123**

Lessons from the case studies: Application of the systems transformation framework 123
Challenges and opportunities in the public sector 127

Annex 1. **Definitions** **131**

Annex 2. **A brief history of systems approaches** **133**

Annex 3. **Case study methodology** **141**

Annex 4. **Interviews conducted for this study** **143**

Figures

Figure 1.1. The Cynefin Framework 16
Figure 1.2. Development of systems thinking: towards methodological pluralism 18
Figure 1.3. Complexity of the American strategy in Afghanistan 18
Figure 1.4. The Vanguard Method 25
Figure 1.5. The development of Scotland's National Performance Framework 31
Figure 2.1. The Ashby Space 47
Figure 2.2. Three complexity regimes 48
Figure 2.3. Picasso's "Bull" lithographs, 1945 51
Figure 2.4. Double Diamond 54
Figure 2.5. The experimentation process 56
Figure 3.1. Domestic violence cases, Suðurnes, 2010-2015 77
Figure 3.2. Together Against Domestic Violence evaluation 79
Figure 3.3. Policy-making cycle 82
Figure 3.4. The experimental policy design model 83
Figure 3.5. Translating the approach to a public sector context: From the Double Diamond
to a table-based simulation 84
Figure 3.6. The top-down, bottom-up approach of experimental culture 86
Figure 3.7. Taxonomy of experiments 86
Figure 3.8. Main features of the funding platform 87
Figure 3.9. The findings of the check phase 97
Figure 3.10. The findings of the plan phase 98
Figure 3.11. Examples of new facilities 100
Figure 3.12. Acute child safety 101
Figure 3.13. Reduction in court measures 103
Figure 3.14. MaRS Solutions Lab's Periodic Table of Systems Change 111
Figure 3.15. Regulatory journeys of taxi drivers 114
Figure 3.16. Regulatory journeys of hoteliers 114
Figure A2.1. Meadows' leverage points 134
Figure A2.2. Les Robinson's Adaptation of Meadows' leverage points 135

Boxes

Box 1.1. Characteristics of wicked problems 14
Box 1.2. Defining systems 17
Box 1.3. The case for system approaches: Ageing populations 19
Box 1.4. Child protection in Greater Amsterdam 26
Box 1.5. The Munro Review of Child Protection 27
Box 1.6. Outcome-based approach to public service reform in Scotland 29
Box 2.1. CoLab's systemic design field guide (Canada) 44
Box 2.2. The search for meaningful measurement in the Early Intervention Foundation ... 62
Box 3.1. A digital development platform for experimentation 87
Box 3.2. Finnish basic income experiment 89
Box 3.3. MaRS Solutions Lab: the road to the sharing economy 109
Box A2.1. Using simulations for obesity, National Collaborative on Childhood Obesity
Research (USA) 135
Box A2.2. Towards methodological pluralism 136

Executive Summary

Governments are increasingly confronted by uncertain and complex challenges whose scale and nature call for new approaches to problem solving. Some governments have started to use systems approaches in policy making and service delivery to tackle complex or "wicked" problems in areas ranging from education to ageing, healthcare and mobility. Systems approaches refer to a set of processes, methods and practices that aim to effect systems change.

Adopting such an approach requires significant adjustments on the part of governments. It means moving away from traditional linear procedures, strategic planning and the notion of reform as an isolated intervention. Instead, policy makers need to focus on building capacity to forecast future scenarios and applying leadership to mobilise a broad range of actors to achieve a common good rather than narrow institutional interests.

Systems approaches help governments to confront problems that traverse administrative and territorial boundaries in a holistic manner. They call for constant adjustment throughout the policy cycle, with implications for the ways in which institutions, processes, skills and actors are organised. Because they focus on outcomes, systems approaches require multiple actors within and across levels of government to work together. To effect systems change, administrations must develop a vision for a desired future outcome, define the principles according to which that future system will operate, and start to implement a set of interventions that will transform the existing system into the future system.

Changing entire systems in the public sector is difficult, largely because public services must be continuously available – they cannot be turned off, redesigned and restarted. Systems approaches can help navigate this difficult transition by allowing new practices to be rolled out while core processes are still running. Furthermore, systems approaches can help organisations to better manage complexity by striking a balance between simplification (focusing on the intended outcome) and complexification (tackling multiple factors within a system at the same time). Changing the system also requires building internal skills into organisations to help them face and adapt to new circumstances.

Systems change invariably spurs debate about the relative value of policy choices, and the trade-offs to be made. For example, in the Canadian case of car-sharing, the flexible transportation system took precedence over other concerns such as precarious work conditions. In Iceland, domestic violence had to be reframed as a public health issue rather than a private matter.

"Independent brokers" can facilitate these value debates and create a level playing field for change. For example, an outside government lab, MaRS Solutions, was involved in changing the Toronto transportation system because all parties viewed it as a non-partisan participant. In Finland, the Nordic think tank Demos Helsinki was able to challenge the *modus operandi* of public sector institutions, thus creating the conditions for introducing experimentation in government.

Initiating and sustaining systems change over time also requires the involvement of senior management, especially when attempting to transform long-established and complex systems. However, leadership is not enough: the participation of a critical mass of actors representing different positions and roles – all of whom understand the need for change and are willing to act on it – is crucial for achieving results. In the Netherlands, the board of directors of the Amsterdam Child and Youth Protection Services supported a change process that lasted for over five years. In Iceland, the heads of police, social services and child protection had to work together to make domestic violence a priority.

Systems approaches require working across organisational boundaries and government levels. For example, in Canada there were concerted efforts at both the municipal and provincial level to help establish a sharing economy. In the Netherlands, although transforming the child protection system began with change in one organisation, it soon became clear that the rest of the supporting structures, from accompanying services to the legal framework, had to be reformed to achieve real results. Once systemic changes are institutionalised it becomes more difficult to return to the "old way of doing things".

Meaningful measurement and feedback mechanisms function as the cornerstones of successful systems change. In policy making there is often a gap between policy design and implementation, especially when addressing complex problems. The case studies highlighted the need for measures that link directly to the *purpose* of systems, such as the Netherlands' approach to child protection and Iceland's risk assessment framework for domestic violence.

Time is an essential resource in systems change: people need to live through and experience the change rather than hearing about it from a third party. The timing of change is thus crucial. In order to implement the Experimental Policy Design programme in Finland, for example, stakeholders had to accelerate their discussions and insert the topic of experimentation into the next government programme during national elections. Both the Dutch and the Icelandic cases illustrate the difficulties of rapidly scaling up change. In order for change to "stick", people need time to internalise the solutions.

Additionally, new, more agile and iterative financing measures must be created to support the use of systems approaches. In the cases of both Canada and Finland, dedicated non-government partners had to invest more time and energy into the projects than was initially planned. In the Dutch case, the initial investment needs exceeded the available resources of the organisation and had to be found elsewhere – though, ultimately, the change produced a 22% reduction in costs per service user. Better instruments are therefore needed to assess the initial return on investment and to track how benefits from systems change are realised and to whom they accrue.

While this report provides some initial insights into the theory and practice of system approaches in the public sector, further work is needed to gather information from relevant experiences and to draw lessons from cases studies in order to develop guidance for policy makers undertaking systems change.

Chapter 1.

Systems approaches in the public sector: From theory to practice

This chapter discusses how systems approaches can deliver value to governments. It starts by discussing why systems approaches are needed in the public sector and why they have not so far been disseminated throughout the sector. The rate of change is continuously increasing and policy makers are confronted with various complex and wicked problems. Systems approaches can be very useful for addressing these problems. Applying a systemic lens to complex problems can help map the dynamics of the surrounding system, explore the ways in which the relationships between system components affect its functioning, and ascertain which interventions can lead to better results. Systems approaches help to demonstrate how systems are structured and how they operate. However, it is not easy to transform public systems. This chapter highlights the main challenges for systems approaches within the public sector: why it is difficult to act under uncertainty, learn from systems adjustments, turn systems off and account for the speed of change in the public sector. The chapter concludes with an overview of the emerging systems thinking practice in the public sector, and explores the question of how systemic approaches have been applied to the transformation of public service delivery.

Introduction

Today, complexity and uncertainty are the norm – they are *contexts*, not just risks. The world seems to operate by a new set of rules are difficult to observe directly. The defence and intelligence communities refer to this state as "VUCA", a reference to the Volatility, Uncertainty, Complexity and Ambiguity characterising geopolitics after the end of the Cold War period. Today, technology, decentralisation, the rise of non-state actors and other factors have accelerated the rise of VUCA in every domain. Labour markets and financial systems are more and more interconnected, making it increasingly difficult to identify the causes and effects of complex problems. For example, a transformative referendum on Brexit seemed unlikely even three years ago; and its cumulative impact on both the United Kingdom and Europe (and indeed the rest of the world) is all but impossible to predict, but will certainly be profound. The public sector as a whole is contending with VUCA, even if administrations do not understand how, where or why.

One key concern is *how best to account for uncertainty while managing greater complexity and still deliver effective services.* To a degree, the answer lies in a policy-making approach that leads to robust systems and adaptive structures. The effectiveness of the decisions made will depend on how completely the problem and its context are understood and how well the dynamic relationship between interventions and context is tolerated. This requires a new mind-set – one that acknowledges uncertainty as part of everyday decision making and encourages working in iterative ways. It also requires an understanding that path dependency[1] exists in all public sector institutions and policy interventions, which may not serve them well, or worse, may lead to predictable outcomes.

Changing the dynamics of a well-established and complicated administrative system is not easy. A new and necessarily complex process of seeing, understanding and deciding is fundamentally challenging our institutions. It has the makings – the foundational conditions – of a *governance crisis*. 19th-century institutions are currently being outmoded by 21st-century problems stemming from interconnectivity, cyber threats, climate change, changing demographic profiles and migration. Public policy makers have traditionally dealt with social problems through discrete interventions layered on top of one another. However, such interventions may shift consequences from one part of the system to another or continually address symptoms while ignoring causes. Recognition of the *complexity gap* (the disconnect between institutional capacity and the problems they face) has therefore led to growing interest in systems thinking and other systems approaches such as design thinking.

Design, systems engineering, systems innovation, systems thinking and design thinking have interlinked philosophical foundations and share, in some cases, methodologies.[2] For this analysis, the umbrella phrase *systems approaches* is used to describe a set of processes, methods and practices that aim to affect systemic change. Using systems approaches in public service delivery can prove challenging due to siloed structures and narrow remits, but can also effect change here too. Public interventions need to move beyond a narrow input-output line of relationships. Of course, the ease or difficulty with which public service delivery systems can be changed depends on the maturity of the system, however new developments are already on the way. These include novel urban transportation systems, e-healthcare systems, learning ecosystems and so on. OECD has drawn attention to this topic in its *Systems Innovation: Synthesis Report* (2015), which discussed public sector challenges through a systems innovation lens.

While the 2015 report relied on specific systems approaches – systems dynamics and socio-technical systems often used in sustainability analyses to explore the role of systems thinking in innovation policy – this report focuses on the ways that public policy makers can use a multitude of systems approaches across different policy areas. OECD (Burns, T. and F. Köster (eds.), 2016; Burns, T., F. Köster and M. Fuster, 2016) has also analysed complexity in the education system with a focus on the importance of different types of learning/building capacity, stakeholder involvement, a "whole of system" vision and trust. Specifically, these publications drew attention to systemic weaknesses in capacity that contribute to today's governance challenges.

System thinking has a long history, but is far from an established field. There are no systematic overviews on the use of systems approaches in the public sector, and the process used in practice is not formalised. Furthermore, little empirical research has been done on the strategies policy makers use to deal with uncertainty in practice. The initial research for this report found only a few well-documented cases of systems approaches in the public sector. The small number may indicate that governments in-source systems capabilities and, thus, tend to rely heavily on outside consultants and designers to lead and instigate systems level changes. Only in recent years has there been renewed interest in applying system approaches, such as design, more rigorously in the public sector.

This report looks at how systems approaches can be used when dealing with complex problems in the public sector. It explores whether, when and why system approaches can deliver value to governments (Chapter 1) and identifies the key principles and tactics involved (Chapter 2). The report aims to provide a platform for discussion to enable decision makers and public services managers to consider the kinds of challenges they face, the resources available to them and what they can expect while engaging in a rigorous problem-solving process using systems approaches. It must be emphasised that no one-size-fits-all solution or systems methodology exists for complex challenges. Solutions – or, more accurately, interventions – and methodologies are highly contextually dependent. The case studies in Chapter 3 shed light on the types of specific preconditions that have enabled some public sector actors to engage with systems approaches.

This report aims to address the following questions: How can I evaluate my own system to see if we require a systems approach? What are the necessary conditions? What variables should be considered when developing a systems approach? As indicated above, there are no simple answers to these questions because each situation is different. However, the following conditions indicate a need for systems approach:

- An "innovation" agenda has taken root in government or a department.

- The inclusion of citizens in decision making has become a priority.

- Citizen orientation is overtaking an institutional orientation.

- There is trust (or demand) in government for experimentation.

- Problems are no longer solved by traditional means (i.e. the line between external stakeholder and government must be blurred to achieve impact).

Important variables include: having a champion committed to change, capacity to experiment, the ability to engage with internal and external stakeholders, and sufficient resources to delay business as usual (time, capital, etc.).

The report examines the use of systems approaches work in two very different contexts typical for governments: first, *a static condition of near paralysis* or a predominantly administrative mode managing well-defined objectives where a change mandate does not exist; and second, *a crisis event* where a change mandate exists, but an understanding of the architecture of the resultant challenge may be fleeting and a transformation process may be unclear. The report encourages the public sector to acknowledge that systems change is necessary and possible in nearly every domain. But, in both static and crisis conditions, administrations need to move away from a procurement-driven policy of using external consultants and contractors to occasionally employ systems approaches, towards allocating resources to make systems approaches an integral part of the public organisations' everyday practice.

Managing complexity in the public sector: The case for systems approaches

Governments have spent decades perfecting systems that can successfully manage *complicated* problems (e.g. banking regulation, trade treaties and healthcare systems), but now find themselves immersed in a world of *complex* problems. A complicated problem is one that is ultimately predictable with sufficient analysis and modelling. Such problems are linear with an identifiable beginning, middle and end; and while they may have many parts it is possible to understand how these collectively create a whole. Management systems such as Six Sigma[3] have demonstrated their value as tools to tackle complicated problems (Kamensky, 2011). Complex problems, on the other hand, are inherently unpredictable. They are frequently referred to as *wicked* or *messy* because it is difficult to assess the true nature of the problem and therefore how to manage it (see Box 1.1). Rather than having discrete parts bound together in linear relationships, complex problems are emergent: they are greater than the sum of their parts.

Box 1.1. Characteristics of wicked problems

The idea of wicked problems emerged in the 1970s from systems theory, and is based on the understanding that problems cannot be understood and addressed in isolation (Head and Alford, 2015; Rittel and Webber, 1973). Wicked problems have many characteristics, but their principal challenge to governments stems from the fact that they cannot be solved by partial or transactional solutions, but instead require concerted, adaptive and carefully stewarded approaches. While there may be different classes of wicked problems (e.g. those arising from path dependencies, incumbent interests and structural lock-ins or accelerated change), each problem has unique traits that stem from its context, history, stakeholders and so on.

The key aspects of wicked problems include the following:

- There are multiple stakeholders, each acting to a certain extent within their own norms.

- Complete diagnosis or understanding is not possible. "There are no definitive definitions" (Hämäläinen, 2015a: 33) because each perspective from which the problem is viewed provides a different understanding of its nature.

- There are no optimum solutions to wicked problems. Nevertheless, long-term options are often discounted in favour of short-term agreements.

- Liminality is inherent in analysis of and intervention in wicked problems. "Liminality" denotes a condition that is "betwixt and between the original positions arrayed by law, custom, convention and ceremony" (Turner, 1977: 95). It refers to a space where regular routines are suspended.

- Because wicked problems are impossible to observe directly, they are unpredictable and their behaviour is uncertain.

Box 1.1. Characteristics of wicked problems *(continued)*

- The efficacy of solutions is difficult to determine because of knock-on effects, self-adaptation and inherent complexity. Attempts have been made with randomised control trials (RCTs) and other evidence-based instruments, but these are fundamentally challenged by the fact that they must be artificially bounded in order to manage complexity and make them feasible (Hämäläinen, 2015b).

Each characteristic on its own would pose significant challenges to traditional governance approaches. But when taken together, they form a disarmingly complex set of obstacles – so much so, that the standard approach for rigid institutions and bureaucracies is to avoid big problems in favour of achievable solutions to proximal issues. Wicked problems require coordinated action on the part of stakeholders (both public and private), adaptability, long-term planning, sustained commitment and active management among other actions. In some cases, these actions are antithetical to administrations, who by design have limited their instruments to work in a linear, unidirectional relationship between problem and solution. However, in an interconnected world where system boundaries are difficult to define, it may no longer be possible to treat any problem as discrete.

Traditional management tools have limited capabilities when applied to complex problems. For the sake of expediency, manageability and clarity, traditional approaches simplify complex problems into what are considered to be their constituent parts and manage them through discrete interventions, layered one on top of another. However, approaches that look at actors and interventions in isolation or disconnected from past efforts may fail to capture and address complex policy legacies. Qualitative case studies have been used to analyse complex problems, as they can treat quantitative and qualitative data comparatively in a narrative structure. However, case studies or more sophisticated methods, such as agent-based simulations, tend to be specific to the problem and context being analysed, and therefore provide little guidance for decision makers seeking to take broader action (ibid.).

As wicked problems continue to multiply, the digital revolution is delivering more power and voice to individual citizens than ever before. Citizens increasingly expect more personalised services that focus on individual needs, while countries now have diverse populations that call for tailor-made approaches. For example, the requirements of elderly care for migrant populations can be vastly different from standard care services.[4] Consequently, standardised, large-scale public service solutions delivered via command and control administrative systems[5] no longer function, forcing government to rethink service delivery boundaries and to design solutions that take into account a broader set of actors and their relationships.

As a result, stakeholder maps have been redrawn. Citizens are now located at or near the centre, not as a contingency but by necessity. Processes that are unable to contend with or adapt to citizen participation will need to be fundamentally reworked (e.g. the Food Standards Agency in the UK reworked its food safety supervisory model based on consumer reports) (OECD, 2016). Public services that are not meaningful or relevant to citizens may struggle to build coalitions of support.

Policy makers must also contend with complex policy legacies. Traditionally reductionist approaches applied to social systems have proven limited in their ability to take into account complex social problems and their web of legacies.

Policy problems have evolved into systemic, interdependent challenges, and their understanding and analysis needs to change accordingly. In highly complex problems, the relationships between cause and effect are neither linear nor simplistic. For example, it might be hard to establish whether reduced waste is a result of improved industrial packaging, changing consumer habits or stricter controls. In this context of boundless complexity, solutions can have serious unintended consequences. For example, the construction of a simple road overpass in Somerville, Massachusetts – which was much needed from an infrastructure development perspective – led to a rise in childhood obesity rates due to part of the community being cut off from leisure and sporting facilities (Curtatone and Esposito, 2014). In complex contexts, cause and effect may only be obvious in hindsight, highlighting the need for different analytical tools.

The Cynefin Framework, developed in the early 2000s by IBM for decision makers, identifies four different contexts: simple, chaotic, complex and complicated (Figure 1.1). In a complicated system there is at least one right answer, as it is possible to identify casual relationships, even if these are not initially visible. However, a complex system is in constant flux. The framework shows that different analytical methods need to be employed to address different policy situations. At the same time, systems in reality are increasingly complex – and not just complicated – and, in expert-driven domains, the mental bias produced by knowing what the right answers should be (seeing systems as complicated and not complex) can produce adverse effects. This means that it is important to understand policy systems better in a public sector context and not overestimate the available knowledge in an increasingly complex world.

Figure 1.1. The Cynefin Framework

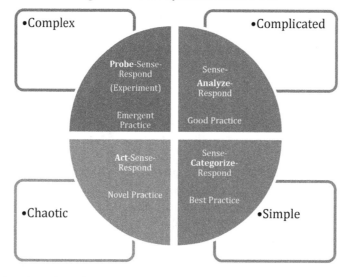

Source: Based on Snowden and Boone (2007).

In essence, systems consist of elements joined together by dynamics that produce an effect, create a whole or influence other elements and systems (see Box 1.2). Systems exist on a spectrum of comprehensibility from the easily observed and analysed (e.g. the food chain) to those that are highly complex or novel requiring postulation (e.g. global climate systems). Systems share some common features: they are usually self-organising meaning that system dynamics grow out of a system's internal structures, they are connected and their parts affect each other, and they are constantly changing and adjusting. They can also be counterintuitive meaning that cause and effect may be distant in time and space. They are governed by feedback and are path-dependent, resistant to change and characterised by non-linear relationships.[6]

Box 1.2. Defining systems

The application of systems approaches depends significantly on how systems are defined (i.e. which relationships are considered important). There are many ways to define systems – geographical proximity (local, regional, national and international), production or markets (e.g. a sectoral system including all upstream and downstream producers and the characteristics of the markets they serve) or technological affinity (technological systems). OECD (2015: 18) has defined systems as "the set of stakeholders who have to interact so that the system as a whole fulfils a specific function (or purpose)". However, this definition may be somewhat misleading, as public policy systems include not only stakeholders, but also regulations, organisational routines, cultural norms and so on. As public policy systems are generally outcome oriented, the present report applies the purposeful systems definition produced by Ackoff and Emery (1972), where the system is bounded and created to achieve its goal(s) and its purpose. Hence, elements of the system are operationalised based on their connection to the goal of the system.

Systems approaches have developed over the last 75 years (see Figure 1.2). Increasing computing power is providing a growing number of tools to trace and visualise causal relationships and simulate complex problems (from causal loop diagrams, stock flows to dynamic simulations, group and mediated modelling). However, modelling comes with a cost: predefined assumptions simplify complex problems and can lead to incorrect assumptions. Qualitative systems approaches have also emerged (soft systems modelling) that concentrate more on identifying the objectives of the system, rather than modelling the system backwards from the predefined goal. Both broad approaches have benefits that can be applied in different policy situations (either as a sense-making tool in a situation where there is an over-abundance of data or to gain insight into decision-making and planning processes). In practice, most systems approaches use a multitude of methods and the origins of the respective approaches are often no longer distinguishable (a more detailed discussion of the theoretical background and limitations of systems thinking can be found in Annex 2).

Applying a systemic lens to complex problems can help map the dynamics of the surrounding system, explore the ways in which the relationships between system components affect its functioning, and ascertain which interventions can lead to better results. Systems thinking helps to demonstrate how systems are structured and how they operate. This requires an understanding of what lies between the different parts, their relationships and the gaps between the knowns. It also means reflecting on how best to use this knowledge to take action (i.e. design and design thinking) by devising proposals to be tested and implemented as system interventions.

A PowerPoint diagram illustrating the US military strategy in Afghanistan from 2009 (Figure 1.3) underscores the fact that visualisation of the system alone does not increase understanding of what needs to be changed in practice. It also emphasises the point that design thinking can help to move from visualising systems to actionable knowledge that allows public managers to make decisions.

Figure 1.2. Development of systems thinking: towards methodological pluralism

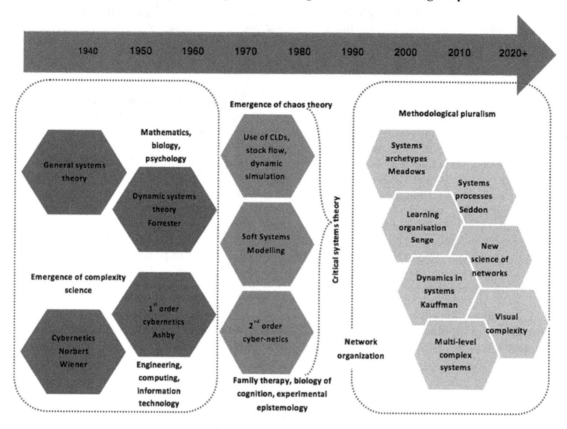

Figure 1.3. Complexity of the American strategy in Afghanistan

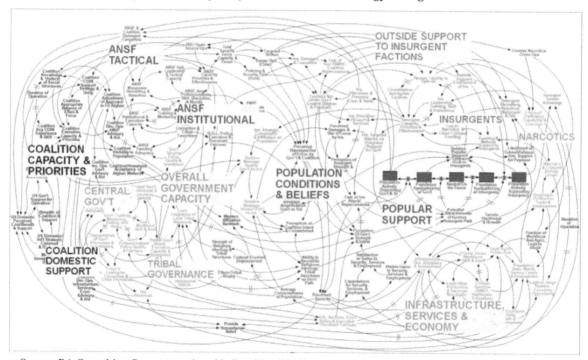

Source: PA Consulting Group, reproduced in Bumiller (2010).

While it is tempting to assume that front-line public services and administrations are distant from or not implicated in large-scale complex problems – let alone wicked problems – careful observation suggests otherwise. For example, responding to the challenge of an aging population requires interventions at the system level to balance social transfer reform and the transformation of service delivery in line with the needs of senior populations (Box 1.3).

Box 1.3. The case for system approaches: Ageing populations

Aging populations are a rich territory for systems approaches. Senior housing, ongoing medical care, nutrition, socialisation and wellbeing services, lifelong learning, mobility and independence are all challenges that benefit from systems approaches, because they sit at the intersection of multiple professional fields, governmental agencies and human needs.

Aging populations in countries like Finland and Japan present a significant challenge for the provision of public services. The pension systems that have guaranteed benefits for decades were designed at a time of an inverted population pyramid, as compared to today. Financial fixes that fall under the clear remit of social service administrations have delayed the failure of pensions, but their future is uncertain as dependency ratios continue to increase in both countries. Tinkering at the system's edges with pension reform, in addition to squeezing additional efficiency out of social services with technology and better management, may continue to preserve the system for some time. However, large-scale systems transformation will be required to prevent the collapse of public budgets. Societies will need to redesign institutions and other structures to meet the demands of a majority senior population. This represents a significant departure from the current state of things which favours the young and economically productive.

This transformation cannot occur overnight. Governments will need to set the stage by working at a systems level to introduce interventions aimed at producing a new societal model that is inclusive of seniors. In other words, a problem that is typically managed at the level of public service delivery now requires administrations to work to transform large-scale systems, in order to avoid further governance crises.

For example, the Centre for Ageing Better (Ageing Better) in the United Kingdom is an independent charitable foundation set up in 2015 to create "a society where everyone can enjoy a good later life" (Centre for Ageing Better, 2017). As one of the UK's What Works Centres, it drives better decision making by generating, sharing and using evidence. Its approach to change is to deliver a whole-system, societal level response to an ageing population. Ageing Better develops, synthesises and applies evidence of what works to enable a good later life, and utilises systems and design thinking to develop and test innovative solutions. The organisation uses its independence to influence both national and local decision makers by communicating information regarding needed changes and working alongside implementation partners to improve later life. Examples of current areas of work include a collaboration with Public Health England to increase awareness and uptake of strength and balance activity, and a partnership with the Greater Manchester Combined Authority to realise their commitment to becoming an age-friendly city region. Ageing Better is currently delivering a programme of insight and co-design work across five localities in Greater Manchester. This work will develop local, regional and national-level interventions to reform the employment support system to better meet the needs of individuals aged over 50 who are unemployed or in low-paid work.

The aging population is not the only domain where system approaches can be applied. Systems approaches can help solve a variety of other public service problems:

- *Mobility*, in general, is a very appropriate field for systems thinking and design, not least because the complex, interdependent systems manifest in physical ways (e.g. in interconnected highway and road networks), but also because the landscape of mobility is shifting away from a need for large-scale infrastructure towards smaller individual or medium-scale solutions that go the "last mile". These represent more complicated problem sets because they are fractal in nature and must correspond very closely with the needs of individual users and their contexts. For example, the City of Warsaw in Poland is developing an urban information system based on micro-transmitters in smartphones for the visually impaired. The system allows smartphone owners to receive written or verbal information, for example, on the location of bus stops, the numbers of arriving trams or the location of a museum entrance (OECD, 2016).

- *Education* is also appropriate for systems approaches due to its contextual variance. Nearly every transaction in education is unique, and the objectives of each participant in the transaction are also unique (e.g. school leader with teacher, teacher with student, student with parent). This makes the system especially resistant to scaling solutions, or those that attempt to apply the same logic to every scenario. Education systems also have compounding and contradictory objectives, such as the inculcation of shared identity versus agency and independence for students. Systems approaches help to navigate this space where the optimal is often impossible.

- *The machinery of government* (i.e. changing the organisational behaviour of agencies) is another space where systems approaches can achieve desired impacts. Design represents a way to organise processes, and bureaucracies, in particular, are repetitive processes. Systems approaches, including design, can function as a neutral broker/arbiter to evaluate processed and work to optimise or, even better, redesign them to enhance their transformative capability.

- *Policing, human services, environmental protection, planning, housing, waste and energy* are all domains in which systems approaches have shown an emerging efficacy. The common denominator is that these services directly interface with the needs and lives of citizens whose expectations and realities have changed under the weight of technological, economic and global change. Societal models formed from institutions, civic practices and expectations, among myriad other factors that served these constituents, are largely outmoded and must be renewed.

Interconnectivity, wicked problems and empowered citizens are all driving governments to change the way in which they work. The systemic nature of today's challenges makes this task much more complex than the government reforms of previous generations. Linear, rigid processes will still have a role in public administration, but the number of transactional processes that these manage will continue to decline. To address the vastly more complex problem sets of this century, systems approaches will have to supplant traditional capabilities. The alternative is waning relevance and a crisis of governance, as citizens look to alternative means to improve their lives.

Challenges of using systems approaches in the public sector

This section explores the following core challenges of using systems approaches in the public sector:

- Balancing the need for evidence with taking action.

- Creating room for open-ended processes and synergistic feedback.

- Changing a system that cannot be turned off, redesigned and restarted because of the need for continuous service provision (e.g. healthcare, education).

- Working amid rapidly changing conditions.

Use of information in highly complex environments: evidence versus action

In the past, decision makers benefited from two forms of complexity reduction: first, a lack of interest, necessity or ability to forecast externalities; and second, simplified classification of information into abstractions or well-delineated silos. This made diagnosis of problems much easier. The availability of less information, especially contradictory information, enabled decision making to proceed unencumbered by uncertainty or complexity.

Today, collecting "enough" data – when full diagnosis of a problem may be too resource intensive or even impossible – is a significant challenge. Sufficiency of information could forever be out of reach. In this context, how do teams proceed with confidence? When working on problems related to broader systems or wicked problems, there is often no definitive answer.

Nevertheless, the wave of evidence-based policy making seems to assume that policy makers are able to wait until a sufficient amount of data is available before acting (Head, 2010: 13). This does not correspond with everyday policy practice, where reforms and "decisive" action are undertaken on a daily basis. This means that, in many cases, policy makers are concentrating on tangible, specific aspects of the puzzle rather than approaching complex problems with a comprehensive, holistic lens. It is indeed unrealistic to hope that every decision in the public sector will be based on robust evidence; however, the associated danger has to be acknowledged as well, as it is difficult to change practices that become commonplace following fast-track decision making.

Conversely, evidence-based methods or rational diagnosis to policy making tend to emphasise positivism and, thus, may become overly technocratic, overlooking the fact that many competing policy solutions are ideological and value based (Stanhope and Dunn, 2011). Thus, information is used not only to diagnose problems, but also to legitimise value-based decisions.

To decrease uncertainty in public sector environments, a variety of methods (e.g. scenario planning, horizon scanning, integrated thinking, etc.) have been used. Nevertheless, uncertainty cannot be reduced in its entirety. Furthermore, governments have become exceedingly dependent on externally produced knowledge; and, yet, there are unavoidable limits to the relevance and usability of knowledge (Mulgan, 2005). In cases where there is an overabundance of information, it may be more important to know which knowledge is not needed for decision making, rather than having information (Feldman and March, 1981: 176).

Learning and adjusting the system: The feedback loop dilemma

Feedback is the core principle in cybernetics: correcting system errors is only possible when systems are capable of obtaining information about the effectiveness of their actions. A feedback loop provides information about the functioning of the systems and may later result in a change in the policy intervention or its effects. Feedback reinforces existing information acquired by the organisation and guides future learning processes both at the individual and organisational levels. Thus, feedback is essential to learning, and most systems approaches talk about single and double-loop learning or even triple-loop learning (Agryris and Schön, 1978; Flood and Romm, 1996). The former describes learning connected directly towards the policy at hand, while the latter refers to a process of reflecting that enables change in the broader management component behind the policy intervention. Another, broader, form of learning is "deutero learning" (learning about learning), which denotes the institutional capacity of organisations to learn (ibid.).

Feedback loops that lead to meaningful insights – and thus, learning – can only be created with open-ended processes. These imply that the system is receptive to alternative ways of doing things, alternative opinions, and has a tolerance for risks and risk-taking (see more in Van Acker and Bouckaert, 2015). Both organisational and individual factors influence these processes. For example, the work of the UK Cross-Government Trial Advice Panel, which supports experimental design in order to understand whether programmes and policies are effective, reflects this need to create feedback loops.

However, such open-ended feedback loops have become more difficult to implement in the public sector, due to the "purchaser-provider split" in public service delivery that emerged with agencification[7] in the public sector and the prevalence of traditional procurement procedures. Procurement practices in the public sector, in general, limit open-ended processes, which also makes the use of iterative, agile methodologies very difficult.[8] There are, however, efforts to counter this: for example, the federal government in the United States has developed a marketplace for agile service delivery by making companies prove their skills with working prototypes on open data, rather than providing lengthy overviews of their qualifications. This minimises "bid and proposal" high-quality vendors, but also diminishes the risks of government entering into open-ended development processes.[9] In many cases, these practices cut the feedback loop to the policy maker and substitute the former with increased accountability. Simple input-output metrics are used as success measures, although these measurement systems assume that accountability equals performance (Kelly, 2005). One drawback is that linear accountability frameworks only work well in predictable environments (Head, 2010: 14).

Static measurement systems that are supposed to supply feedback to dynamic processes in the public sector tend not to work.[10] Most evaluation systems in the public sector do not account for long lead times or complex feedback loops permeating processes surrounding wicked problems. In these cases, where measurement is difficult, feedback starts to depend on stakeholders and their value-based judgements. Consequently, feedback related to complex issues needs to also incorporate the dynamic nature of processes – continually "learning by doing" – as well as systems knowledge and the ability to place value-based information into context. This is essential in order to quickly address ripple effects in the system and unintended consequences – such as recognising that building a road overpass has had a serious effect on children's health (Curtatone and Esposito, 2014).

Turning a system off

New systems models can be designed in the abstract, but ultimately need to be built within existing systems. This is because large-scale systems providing services such as education or healthcare cannot be turned off, redesigned and restarted as a company might shut down an underperforming vehicle plant to replace outdated equipment. This problem recalls March's (1991) dilemma of exploring and exploiting: how to introduce systemic change while at the same time providing services described by laws and regulations (see also the discussion in Lember, Kattel and Tõnurist, 2016).

Most public services must be continuously available. For public sector innovators this makes for a particularly perplexing class of problem. Inherent complexity and interconnectedness form part of the state's basic function, which means that the shape of such public services must be preserved. While Buckminster Fuller's instruction to "build a new model that makes the existing model obsolete" is empowering, many public services cannot be made obsolete in the face of this kind of "wicked" problem. They can and should be renewed, but their core function must remain constant. This structural dilemma requires a non-standard approach, because any intervention aimed at transformation must be at once sympathetic *and* disruptive to the old system; incrementalism must be married to a whole systems framework.

Take education, for example – perhaps the most reform-intensive domain in the public sector portfolio. Nearly every corner of most education systems is targeted for reform, yet little systematic improvement is being realised. Why? How can the United States, for example, spend on average USD 600 billion per year on public education and nearly the same sum on reform of that system, and still see student performance stagnant or declining?

There are at least two reasons for education's resistance to large-scale change beyond the fundamental issue of its character as an enterprise highly determined by its multivalent context (location, parents, teachers, students, curriculum, etc.). First, the system cannot be turned off and rebuilt. Every day, students show up in classrooms with real demands for learning and, increasingly, emergent needs for additional social services. Their needs must be met. Moreover, most students and parents are unwilling to be a test case for reform. Change must happen in an incremental, step-wise fashion that gives administrators and other stakeholders' confidence that the effort will lead to improvement. In Finland, for instance, the national curriculum is renewed on a ten-year cycle and, in the last round (2016), was organised to include the opinions of as many stakeholders as possible. While Finland's curriculum is the product of an exemplary education policy and development process, it is also the product of a system that is continuously operative and resistant to change. A decade-long multi-stakeholder process would seem glacial compared to systems change in the tech sector, for example. Second, authority in most education systems is largely concentrated in central offices and other administrative bodies. In most cases, the system is designed around the people that run the system itself, rather than the "clients" (i.e. students). This means that those who are responsible for maintenance and continuity of the system must also manage its reform and foster innovative new practices. However, their interests tend to run contrary to their own needs. Debate about education's purpose and shape in the future is unusual if not altogether absent in this administrative format. Without a clear idea about what the future should be and why, it is difficult to organise reform efforts around common goals. In other words, change cannot be systemic; it is always piecemeal and therefore unable to achieve the synergistic effects promised and demonstrated by systems approaches. Attempts are being made at rendering the "existing model obsolete", such as with the charter school movement in the United States, but these remain marginal and have not achieved the promised transfer of innovation to traditional education settings.

Designers and systems thinkers, and those responsible for improving public services, should ask themselves critical questions about how to keep core services running while reforming the underlying system. They should work to uncover what is working well in a system and should be preserved and, similarly, what rigidities and frictions exist that work against change, but are important to preserving the public interest. Furthermore, it is important to know whether it is possible to work within the system to achieve reform or whether it is necessary to approach change from the outside as well. Transformative change may also require the spark of a crisis in order to significantly redesign an entrenched system.

All of this, of course, takes time and is akin to changing the tyres while driving a car. In government, time is a scarce resource principally because of the instability caused by political life cycles. This perennial challenge cannot be fully addressed here, but suffice it to say that a widely shared vision for the future of a system born out of a co-creative process – as opposed to a set of administrative priorities – will go a long way to providing a durable platform for systems change.

Speed of change

Established institutions promote their own stability; they are by-and-large path-dependent and can be highly resistant to change. Any ministry whose origins date back a century or more will likely combine remits that no longer make sense today. For example, in Finland, the Ministry of Transport and Communications (LVM) exemplified a combinatory logic compatible with a time when transportation and communications infrastructure were developed simultaneously. But today, transportation and communications (ICT) are moving closer to each other. Nevertheless, the concept of "transportation as a service" with a well-functioning communication infrastructure is emerging (LVM, 2016). Robotisation and self-driving vehicles are also transforming the transportation ecosystem in this direction (Pilli-Sihvola et al., 2015). While the problems the public sector faces today have changed considerably, established public institutions still struggle to change. This is one of the core challenges of systems thinking in the public sector. It is critical to understand this issue, as prior analyses have shown that changing the architecture of the system can have a more profound impact than discrete policy interventions following an ad hoc diagnosis of policy failures (see OECD, 2015: 43 for references).

Systems approaches to public service delivery: Approaches and emerging evidence

The introduction to this chapter discussed the application of system lenses to complex challenges faced by the public sector. Here, the report explores the question of how systemic approaches have been applied to the transformation of public service delivery.

There have been several proponents of system thinking in the public sector,[11] as well as in connection with the development and application of management theories to public service delivery. The shift in interest to system approaches is linked to the understanding of citizens as an integral part of service delivery as "co-producers" or "co-creators", who possess important information on the performance of the system.

While no discrete list of characteristics exists for good service delivery in the public sector, some elements have been outlined in the literature. These include: knowing the service users (their requirements, expectations, etc.), having a user-focused mind-set, designing services according to service users' needs and measuring success from the viewpoint of end-users (Osborne, Radnor and Nasi, 2013: 139). However, a focus on reforming discrete elements of public service delivery systems (in connection to the service-dominant logic)[12] has also been critiqued, as more profound system-level problems are not brought to light (Jung, 2010; Powell et al., 2010). This is especially important in the public sector, due to the increasingly fragmented and inter-organisational context of public service delivery, where systems have become more complex and problems more difficult to deal with (Osborne, Radnor and Nasi, 2013: 135). This means that changing the service delivery system for a single public sector organisation or an agency may not deliver the desired effect.

One example of systems thinking applied to service delivery is the Vanguard Method (following Seddon's "Check-Plan-Do" cycle) developed for use in service organisations. This method identifies two different types of demand in service organisations: *value demand* (what the organisation is asked to do or provide/which problems to solve) and *failure demand* (demand caused by failure to provide the right service or product to the customer). This model starts by identifying the purpose in user terms and quality demand. It then moves to checking capabilities and rebuilds the system in ways to eliminate redundancies and "waste" and focuses on the processes that generate value for the user (see Figure 1.4).

Figure 1.4. The Vanguard Method

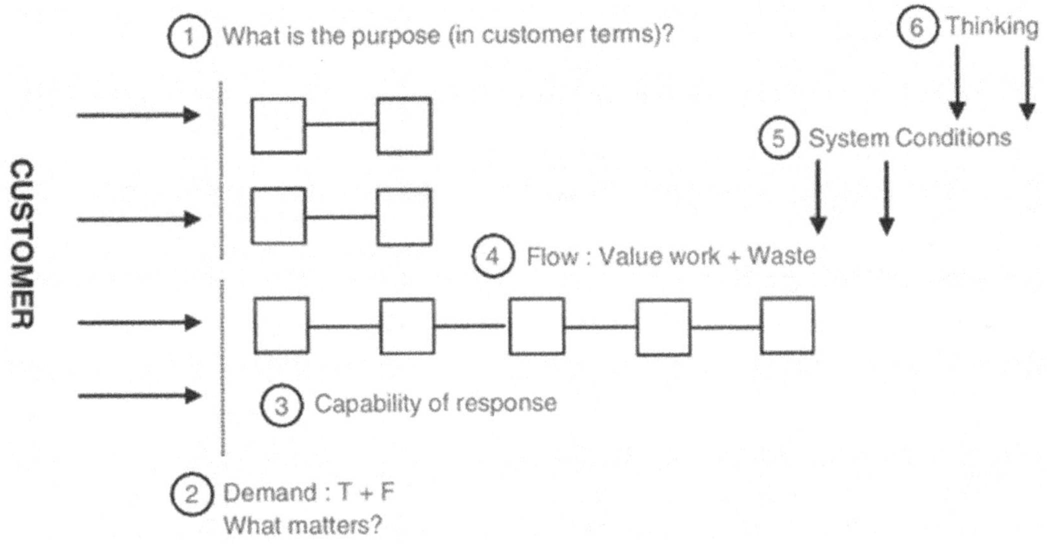

Source: Seddon (2003: 112).

The Vanguard Method has been applied to public sector organisations. For example, the case study in Chapter 3 dealing with child protection in the Netherlands shows that implementing systematic change in the public sector takes time, but can have very positive outcomes (see Box 1.4). The Vanguard Method, in particular, gives practitioners a chance to undergo individual learning processes that are necessary in order to change their institutional processes.

Box 1.4. Child protection in Greater Amsterdam

Jeugdbescherming Regio Amsterdam (Child and Youth Protection Services in the Amsterdam area, CYPSA) is the public youth protection agency of Amsterdam. Each year, it looks after 10 000 at-risk children with the help of 600 staff. In 2008, the agency was placed under heightened supervision by the inspection services and the Amsterdam alderman because it was unable to fulfil its core mission: assessing risks posed to vulnerable children and providing timely help. In 2011, a large-scale redesign of the organisation was initiated with the designated aim of keeping "Every child safe". A core group of ten caseworkers, two team managers, two psychologists and a consultant trained in the Vanguard Method were given the authority to redesign internal processes.

Over a period of three months, the group conducted the "check", "plan" and "do" phases of the Vanguard Method and delivered a working approach ("doing" what was "planned"). The check showed that CYPSA was split organisationally across different roles: social workers working with parents on a voluntary basis, guardians who had legal responsibility over children and parole officers working together with convicted juvenile offenders. As a result, there was no one single contact point for families. Case workers were therefore unsure who should act on signals of risk to children. Instead, they worked with established protocols and forms of reporting that were not central to the mission at hand – keeping children safe. The planning phase established new principles of action and outlined phases of engagement. Case workers would deal with the whole family system and communicate directly with families (the "Functional Family Parole Services"). Previous silos were to be abolished and replaced with teams organised around potential cases. A focus was placed on early intervention and holistic care of the entire family.

After the initial analysis, three teams of volunteers were given three weeks to complete the process and simultaneously undergo their own learning process. This was followed by a "rolling-in" stage during which 40 teams were taken through the process to experience their own "check", "plan" and "do" phases. This lasted a full year and required additional changes to supporting services such as IT, facilities and so on.

The whole process exceeded initial expectations: it improved both the quality of the public service and diminished the associated costs. The number of cases where children had to be forcibly removed from families decreased by 50%. The changes reportedly resulted in annual cost savings of EUR 30 million. In 2015, CYPSA was elected the Best Public Sector Organisation in the Netherlands (see Chapter 3 for more details of this case study).

Source: Wauters and Drinkgreve (2016).

While there is case-specific evidence that systems approaches (including the Vanguard Method) have been applied in the public sector, there are no systematic reviews of their success or failure. Public sector organisations tend not to make available the specificities of reform processes. Consequently, there is also a lack of research regarding which specific systems approaches fit a specific context. Nevertheless, systems approaches have been applied across a variety of fields in social research and action research. For example, systems thinking has been applied to address issues including:

- Childhood obesity and social policy in Australia (Allender et al., 2015; Canty-Waldron, 2014).

- Child protection in England (Lane, Munro and Husemann, 2016).

- Design/management of children's services in England and Wales (Gibson and O'Donovan, 2014).

- Health prevention including obesity and tobacco,[13] mental health services in North Wales (Evans et al., 2013) and public health more generally[14] (WHO has applied systems thinking to health systems reform) (WHO, 2009).

- Higher education in the United Kingdom (Dunnion and O'Donovan, 2014).

- Environmental follow-up in Sweden (Lundberg, 2011), waste oil management in Finland (Kapustina et al., 2014.) and sustainable food consumption in Norway (Vittersø and Tangeland, 2015).

- Infrastructure planning in Australia (Pepper, Sense and Speare, 2016).

- Military and political affairs in the United States (de Czege, 2009).

One of the most well-known systems exercises in the public sector is the Munro Review of Child Protection (see Box 1.5). It utilised a multitude of systems approaches without devising a concrete methodology (in comparison to the Vanguard Method), with the aim of showing how different reforms interact and the effects on the system's objectives before developing a narrative account to explain what needs to be changed. While the review received broad coverage in the media and positive reactions from practitioners, implementing the recommendations was not straightforward. The process was time-consuming and complex, as the involvement of many actors was necessary to change public policy systems. For example, during the process of organisational redesign it may be necessary to transfer authority from one organisation to another. In the public sector context, this often requires legislative changes (as was the case with the Munro Review). These issues can become magnified if problems fall between municipal and state mandates. For example, it can be very difficult to plan working transportation systems across municipal boundaries to take into account desired moving patterns.

Box 1.5. The Munro Review of Child Protection

One of the most well-known examples of systems thinking in the public sector is the Munro Review of Child Protection in England. In 2010, the Department of Education commissioned Professor Eileen Munro to perform an independent review with a view to reforming the child protection system. The goals were to understand why policies were not yielding the desired results (protecting children from abuse and neglect) and to design a system of child protection based upon the new insights.

The central question in the analysis was: "What elements can help professionals make the best possible judgements to protect vulnerable children?" The analysis demonstrated that the system had become overly bureaucratic and focused on compliance rather than the welfare and safety of children. In other words, the system was working in service of itself rather than its "clients".

The Munro Review was published in several stages. In 2010, a "Systems Analysis" of the current child protection system was published. This was purposely analytical and aimed at policy makers. It showed how reforms interact and the effect these interactions were having on institutional practices. In 2011, a second report entitled "The Child's Journey" traced children's experience in the system from needing to receiving help. The report also underlined the need to work with children and families who have not yet met the threshold for child protection. Following extensive consultation, a final report detailed how to develop a more child-centred system of child protection together with a flexible assessment system.

Box 1.5. The Munro Review of Child Protection *(continued)*

The review used causal loop diagrams (CLDs) to communicate how causal relationships in the child protection system worked, and to visualise how the "compliance culture" had evolved. Several other concepts from systems theory were also used in the review including single and double-loop learning, ripple effects, requisite variety and socio-technical systems, among others.

Following publication of the review, the Secretary of State for Education issued eight trials based on its recommendations. These resulted in unintended consequences due to exogenous factors including rocketing caseloads and public sector cuts (Munro and Lushey, 2012). Further roll-out of the system was postponed due to government delays in changing statutory guidance.

Sources: Munro 2010, 2011a, 2011b.

Research shows that without proper training and clear guidelines, practitioners return to previous delivery models, even if systems approaches are used to re-evaluate public service conditions (see Carey et al., 2015: 4). Although this is essentially human nature, such unwillingness to embrace new ways of working continues to be one of the biggest barriers to change in the public sector (NAO, 2006). Active resistance to change and political lobbying against reform also comes from powerful incumbents, as has been noted in the case of the energy sector.

The broader public sector change and innovation literature highlight several factors that can inhibit systems change in the public sector. These include: unwillingness among managers to take risks (e.g. Osborne and Brown, 2011; Torugsa and Arundel, 2015), possible political scrutiny from opposing parties (Potts and Kastelle, 2010), short-term delivery pressures, organisational culture in the public sector and low levels of management autonomy (Bysted and Jespersen, 2014; Lægreid, Roness and Verhoest, 2011). Prominent systems thinker, Jake Chapman, has outlined some of the characteristics linked to systems failure in policy making (Chapman 2002: 13):

- aversion to failure
- pressure for uniformity of public services
- perception that command and control is the best way to exercise power
- lack of evaluation of previous policies
- lack of time
- tradition of secrecy
- siloed systems and dominance of turf wars
- complicated procurement systems that limit experimentation
- loss of professional integrity and autonomy under the knife of efficiency.

Not all of these factors are uniformly applicable across the public sector. For example, some countries exhibit a higher level of discretionary learning (staff taking responsibility and exercising agency to solve problems), which helps to introduce bottom-up systems-level change (Arundel, Casali and Hollanders, 2015; Kaasa 2013). Likewise, institutions that are not mature or still developing are more receptive to change, making fundamental systems-level change more likely in administrative contexts with less path dependencies. Practitioners and public sector managers usually have little control over organisational culture after it has segmented or become institutionalised, so existing systems or even policy capacity can be a pre-determining factor for instigating systems-level change. In addition, different government functions divided into a "silo system" can have large path dependencies, which become a large barrier to changing public service delivery systems (Bason, 2010). Hence, many public sector organisations are ill equipped to deal with new, complex and wicked problems.

Such contextual problems raise key questions: Is there room for systems approaches in the public sector? How can systems change be introduced into the public sector? Only a handful of surveys have explored these questions. In 2001, a US survey showed that 50% of innovations were initiated by front-line staff and middle managers, 70% arose in response to a crisis and 60% resulted specifically from austerity measures (Borins, 2001). In many cases, political opportunities to create momentum for systems-level change result from crises (McCann, 2013), which in turn drives innovation and change in the public sector (Kay and Goldspink, 2012). Both the physical emergence of crises and the perceived threat or public uproar can function as a window of opportunity to use systems approaches to reconfigure public service systems and policy on a larger scale. Crises tend to suspend the rules and norms that limit experimentation. Most importantly, a crisis can be an opportunity to step back and ask questions about the core purposes of programmes or services. By questioning and reasserting purpose, an administration creates an opportunity to redesign not only services, but how those services are resourced, managed and renewed if and when the crisis recedes.

Box 1.6. Outcome-based approach to public service reform in Scotland

In 2007, the Scottish National Party won the Scottish Parliamentary election for the first time. The party gained 47 seats and decided to form a minority government. This meant that the government had to find a larger consensus base to implement policy reforms. The government decided to reform its structure and adopt an outcome-based approach, later termed the Scottish Approach to Public Service Reform. While the process cannot be described as a systems approach, it had the characteristics of a broader systems-level change.

The reform effort started by identifying universal goals across government. These discussions were held among the top leadership comprising a small circle of senior civil servants and politicians. This process led to agreement on 14 vision statements describing the Scotland the leadership wanted to build. By necessity, these statements were broad and all-embracing and, as such, were difficult to dispute. The statements were transformed into formal national outcomes, which form the backbone of the National Performance Framework (NPF). There are currently 16 national outcomes which are widely accepted in Scotland:

- We live in a Scotland that is the most attractive place for doing business in Europe.
- We realise our full economic potential with more and better employment opportunities for our people.
- We are better educated, more skilled and more successful, renowned for our research and innovation.
- Our young people are successful learners, confident individuals, effective contributors and responsible citizens.
- Our children have the best start in life and are ready to succeed.
- We live longer, healthier lives.

Box 1.6. Outcome-based approach to public service reform in Scotland *(continued)*

- We have tackled the significant inequalities in Scottish society.

- We have improved the life chances for children, young people and families at risk.

- We live our lives safe from crime, disorder and danger.

- We live in well-designed, sustainable places where we are able to access the amenities and services we need.

- We have strong, resilient and supportive communities where people take responsibility for their own actions and how they affect others.

- We value and enjoy our built and natural environment and protect it and enhance it for future generations.

- We take pride in a strong, fair and inclusive national identity.

- We reduce the local and global environmental impact of our consumption and production.

- Our people are able to maintain their independence as they get older and are able to access appropriate support when they need it.

- Our public services are high quality, continually improving, efficient and responsive to local people's needs.

These broad outcomes made it necessary to work across government silos. It soon became clear that success depended on changing the structure of government administration. This led to the abolition of department structures in the Scottish Government. Ministries were reformed in line with the responsibility areas of the national outcomes.

Following the leadership-focused start of the reform process, the government took a partnership-centred approach across central and local government and public services. Specific goals and key stakeholders were identified for each policy area under the national outcomes. Three main elements were emphasised to achieve the goals: (i) assets and strengths of individuals and communities; (ii) co-production of policies with people; and (iii) improvement in the local ownership of data to drive change. This signified a move within public services from top-down, service-led, reactive delivery towards more personalised, preventative and collaborative ways of working. Broader-based workshops followed to identify more concrete outcomes and measurement indicators under different national outcomes. Thus, the overarching NPF is strengthened by a list of detailed outcomes frameworks operating at local and national levels. To promote the change process at the local level, the government adopted a 3-Step Improvement Framework for Scotland's Public Services outlining the guiding principles to help achieve improvements in different outcome areas.

The reform process was successful in creating a common vision at the national level and inspiring new initiatives at the local level. It recognised complexity and the necessity of change and innovation. Nevertheless, the interviewed experts noted that much of the reform effort was guided by measurement efforts. Initially, 45 indicators were set to accompany the national outcomes in the NPF. These were supposed to enable the government and the public to track progress towards the national outcomes. While the government tried to move away from targets, inputs and outputs, this proved difficult. Many outcomes (e.g. community engagement, cohesion, trust, social connectedness/capital, etc.) were difficult to measure, which necessitated a reliance on proxies and led to problems with establishing the effect policy activities had on changes in indicators.

Box 1.6. Outcome-based approach to public service reform in Scotland *(continued)*

For example, the government wanted to measure "how well families were nurturing their children". In the absence of specifically developed indicators, the reform process used dental checks of children (which have been linked to more nurturing families). However, this indicator does not measure the domain the government actually wanted to influence. Meaningful measurement and the ways in which it supports outcome-oriented activities (and not only accountability) has been the main area of critique regarding this approach. The recent What Works position paper (Cook, 2017) noted – among other suggestions – that the approach needs to maximise not only the learning from outcomes, but also the method by which these outcomes are delivered. The approach needs to be tailored to the context of the purpose, which means that the collected data have to be meaningful and measurable for the purpose and use multiple forms of evidence.

With that said, the Scottish Government has been continuously improving the NPF. It was revised in 2011 to reflect lessons learned during the previous government and the priorities outlined in different review documents (e.g. Manifesto Commitments, the Government Economic Strategy, Programme for Government and Spending Review documents). A key change was the expansion of indicator sets to 50 indicators. In 2015, a broader engagement process was initiated with 15 indicator workshops involving external stakeholders from sectors including health and social care, the built environment, justice and communities, children and families, economy and skills, culture and external affairs. As of 2017, there are 55 national outcome indicators and greater attention is being paid to review of the framework.

Figure 1.5. The development of Scotland's National Performance Framework

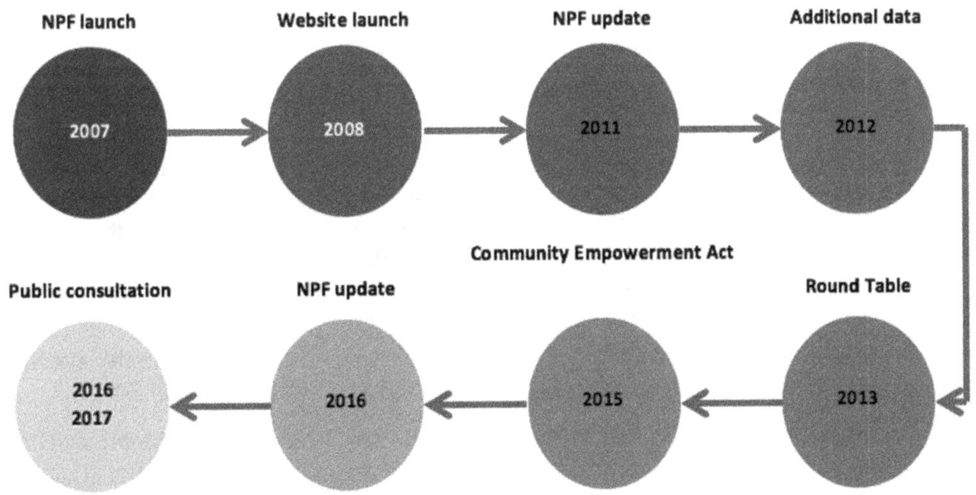

Sources: Cook. (2017); Scottish Government (2016).

However, systems approaches should function as a continuous, dialogic process. Policy makers should not wait for political crisis to implement change. Business-as-usual conditions should provide opportunities to implement systems approaches in the public sector. Regardless of the different types of public sector organisations and context, there is evidence that policy entrepreneurs – committed leaders – can create space for change in any institutional context (Leonard, 2010). It has also proven possible to overcome budget and temporal uncertainty and restrictions if practitioners have the will to work towards the transformation of a system (Torugsa and Arundel, 2015). Personal leadership and commitment on the part of key individuals is an important factor in supporting successful change in the public sector (Pärna and von Tunzelmann, 2007), even if this occurs in a piecemeal fashion. What matters is that work towards systems change is initiated and sustained as fully as possible. Strategies that open up organisations and support outside collaboration with enterprises and citizens also enforce organisational learning, and help speed up and spread the adoption of change (Walker, 2013). Nevertheless, broader engagement with systems approaches may require a substantive shift in the culture and operations of public organisations.

Notes

1   Path dependency is a concept of historical institutionalism conveying an extended time period of considerable stability in public policymaking – persistence of policy trajectory – that may be punctuated by turbulent, formative moments (Peters et al., 2005).

2   A useful shorthand is to think of the phrase "systems thinking" as describing the ability to understand the properties and dynamics of complex systems. Its increasingly popular twin, "design thinking", generally describes the process of ordering information in complex systems in such a way that leads to action.

3   "Six Sigma is a technique for improving process quality originally developed by Motorola in the U.S. in 1986 and later adopted on a large scale and popularized by firms such as General Electric. The name Six Sigma derives from the statistical probability of an error rate (or a defect rate in the case of manufacturing) outside of six standard deviations from the mean ... Motorola and others firms have developed certification procedures for training people in Six Sigma techniques that result in various levels of certification such as black belt, green belt, etc. Currently, Six Sigma is used in many firms and different sectors of industry" (Verma, 2012: 7-8).

4   Draulans and De Tavernier (2016) analysed the care needs of older people in Turkish communities in Belgium. They showed that traditional public service delivery systems do not work for individuals from a different cultural background, who tend to be ignored by the system. New policy networks and approaches are needed to reach people from different communities.

5   "Command and control administration" refers to a traditional, hierarchical planning model (see Seddon, 2008).

6   See WHO (2009) in the case of health systems.

7   Agencification describes the process of creating semi-autonomous agencies operating at arm's length from the government administration within the public sector, as part of the New Public Management (NPM) reforms since the 1980s (Overman and Van Thiel, 2016).

8   Public sector organizations normally use some form of fixed price contracts in which time, cost and scope of activity are fixed in the procurement process. This usually means that the supplier takes the brunt of the risk at the forefront, and changing activities based on feedback and "learning by doing" becomes very difficult later on. This is easily exemplified in software development processes (Book, Gruhn and Striemer, 2012).

9   See the case study on Micro-purchase Platform in OECD (2017: 99).

10   In the context of public sector innovation measurement, see Kattel et al. (2015).

11   These include Jake Chapman at Demos in the United Kingdom, and John Seddon with lean systems (under Vanguard Consulting) and the more detailed Vanguard Method. Recently, NESTA and other think tanks/policy labs have discussed the use of systems thinking within the public sector in the context of public sector innovation. Donella Meadows' work has also been used in the public sector context, but her perspective on systems theory and, in particular, leverage points was not specifically developed with public service delivery in mind.

12   Osborne, Radnor and Nasi (2013) argue that public management theory is changing towards a "fit-for-purpose" approach, which sees public services as services, with a distinctive service-dominant logic and managerial challenges. This implies a rejection of previously applied product-dominant public management theory. A service-dominant approach places "activities driven by specialized knowledge and skills, rather than units of output, at the centre of exchange processes" (Lusch and Vargo, 2006: 55).

13   See the overview of obesity policy in Bures et al. (2014), and Johnston, Matteson and Finegood (2014).

14   See the review of relevant papers in Carey et al. (2015).

References

Ackoff, R.L. and F.E. Emery (1972), On Purposeful Systems: An Interdisciplinary Analysis of Individual and Social Behaviour as a System of Purposeful Events. Tavistock, London, UK.

Allender, S. et al. (2015), "A community based systems diagram of obesity causes", *PloS one*, Vol. 10/7, pp. 1-12.

Arundel, A., L. Casali and H. Hollanders (2015), "How European public sector agencies innovate: The use of bottom-up, policy-dependent and knowledge-scanning innovation methods", *Research Policy*, Vol. 44, pp. 1271-1282.

Bason, C. (2010), Leading Public Sector Innovation: Co-creating for a Better Society. Policy Press, Bristol, UK.

Book, M., V. Gruhn and R. Striemer (2012), "adVANTAGE: A fair pricing model for agile software development contracting", *Agile Processes in Software Engineering and Extreme Programming*, 111, pp. 193-200.

Borins, S. (2001), *The Challenge of Innovating in Government.* PricewaterhouseCoopers Endowment for the Business of Government, Arlington, VA, www.strategie-cdi.ro/spice/admin/UserFiles/File/CA%20The%20Challenge%20of%20innovating%20in%20government.pdf.

Bures, R.M. et al. (2014), "Systems science: A tool for understanding obesity", *American Journal of Public Health*, Vol. 104, p. 1156.

Burns, T. and F. Köster (eds.) (2016), *Governing Education in a Complex World*, OECD Publishing, Paris. http://dx.doi.org/10.1787/9789264255364-en

Burns, T., F. Köster and M. Fuster (2016), *Education Governance in Action: Lessons from Case Studies*, OECD Publishing, Paris. http://dx.doi.org/10.1787/9789264262829-en

Bysted, R. and K.R. Jespersen (2014), "Exploring managerial mechanisms that influence innovative work behaviour: Comparing private and public employees", *Public Management Review*, Vol. 16/2, pp. 217-241.

Canty-Waldron, J. (2014), "Using systems thinking to create more impactful social policy", *Journal of Futures Studies*, Vol. 19/2, pp. 61-86.

Carey, G. et al. (2015), "Systems science and systems thinking for public health: A systematic review of the field", *BMJ Open*, Vol. 5/12, p. e009002.

Centre for Ageing Better (2017), Case Study Submission for OECD Paper "Working with Change: Systems Approaches to Public Sector Challenges".

Chapman, J. (2002), System Failure: Why Governments Must Learn to Think Differently (2nd edn). Demos, London.

Cook, A. (2017), *Outcome Based Approaches in Public Service Reform*. Position Paper. What Works Scotland, Glasgow, Scotland, http://whatworksscotland.ac.uk/wp-content/uploads/2017/04/OutcomeBasedApproachesinPublicServiceReform.pdf.

Curtatone, J.A. and M. Esposito (2014), "Systems thinking: A better way to make public policy", *Governing*, 18 August 2014, www.governing.com/gov-institute/voices/col-systems-thinking-public-policy-programs.html.

de Czege, H.W.U.A. (2009), "Systemic operational design: Learning and adapting in complex missions", *Military Review*, Vol. 89/1, p. 2.

Draulans, V. and W. De Tavernier (2016), "Vanaf mijn tiende een sandwichkind. Intergenerationele zorg en samenwonen in de Genkse Turkse gemeenschap" [Intergenerational care and cohabitation in the Genk Turkish community], in D. Luyten, K. Emmery, E. Mechels (eds.), *Gezinnen, Relaties en Opvoeding, Vol. 1, Zoals het klokje thuis tikt. Samenhuizen van volwassen kinderen met hun ouders*. Garant, Antwerp, Belgium, pp. 83-99.

Dunnion, J. and B. O'Donovan (2014), "Systems thinking and higher education: The Vanguard Method", *Systemic Practice and Action Research*, Vol. 27/1, pp. 23-37.

Evans, S. et al. (2013), "System-level change in mental health services in North Wales: An observational study using systems thinking", *International Journal of Social Psychiatry*, pp. 337-351.

Feldman, M.S. and J.G. March (1981), "Information in organizations as signal and symbol", *Administrative Science Quarterly*, Vol. 26/2, pp. 171-186.

Flood, R.L. and N.R. Romm (1996), "Contours of diversity management and triple loop learning", *Kybernetes*, Vol. 25/7/8, pp. 154-163.

Gibson, J. and B. O'Donovan (2014), "The Vanguard Method as applied to the design and management of English and Welsh Children's Services departments", *Systemic Practice and Action Research*, Vol. 27/1, pp. 39-55.

Hämäläinen, T.J. (2015a), "Governance solutions for wicked problems: Metropolitan innovation ecosystems as frontrunners to sustainable well-being", *Technology Innovation Management Review*, Vol. 5/10, pp. 31-41.

Hämäläinen, T. (2015b), How to Deal with Growing Complexity and Uncertainty? How can Decision-makers Deal with Increasingly Complex and Uncertain Systems? 14 August 2015. SITRA, Helsinki, www.sitra.fi/en/blogs/weekly-notes-week-33-how-deal-growin-complexity-and-uncertainty-0.

Head, B.W. (2010), "How can the public sector resolve complex issues? Strategies for steering, administering and coping", *Asia-Pacific Journal of Business Administration*, Vol. 2/1, pp. 8-16.

Head, B.W. and J. Alford (2015), "Wicked problems implications for public policy and management", *Administration & Society*, Vol. 47/6, pp. 711-739.

Johnston, L.M., C.L. Matteson and D.T. Finegood, (2014), "Systems science and obesity policy: A novel framework for analyzing and rethinking population-level planning", *American Journal of Public Health*, Vol. 104/7, pp. 1270-1278.

Jung, T. (2010), "Citizens, co-producers, customers, clients, captives? A critical review of consumerism and public services", *Public Management Review*, Vol. 12, 439-446.

Kaasa, A. (2013), "Culture as a possible factor of innovation: Evidence from the European Union and neighbouring countries", *SEARCH Working Paper*. European Commission, Brussels.

Kamensky, J.M. (2011), "Managing the complicated vs. the complex", *The Business of Government Magazine*, Fall/Winter/2011, pp. 66-70, www.businessofgovernment.org/sites/default/files/JohnKamensky.pdf.

Kapustina, V. et al. (2014), "System analysis of waste oil management in Finland", *Waste Management and Research*, Vol. 32/4, pp. 297-303.

Kattel, R. et al. (2014), "Can we measure public sector innovation? A literature review", *LIPSE Working Papers*, 2, 1-45.

Kay, R. and C. Goldspink (2012), What Public Sector Leaders Mean When They Say They Want to Innovate. Incept Labs, Sydney, Australia.

Kelly, J.M. (2005), "The dilemma of the unsatisfied customer in a market model of public administration", *Public Administration Review*, Vol. 65/1, pp. 76-84.

Kingdon, J.W. (1995), *Agendas, Alternatives, and Public Polocoes*. HarperCollins College Publishers, New York.

Lægreid, P., P.G. Roness and K. Verhoest (2011), "Explaining the innovative culture and activities of state agencies", *Organization Studies*, Vol. 32/10, pp. 1321-1347.

Lane, D.C., E. Munro and E. Husemann (2016), "Blending systems thinking approaches for organisational analysis: Reviewing child protection in England", *European Journal of Operational Research*, Vol. 251/2, pp. 613-623.

Lember, L., R. Kattel and P. Tõnurist (2016), "Public administration, technology and administrative capacity", *Working Papers in Technology Governance and Economic Dynamics*, Vol. 72, pp. 1–30.

Leonard, D.K. (2010), "Pockets of effective agencies in weak governance states: Where are they likely and why does it matter?", *Public Administration and Development*, Vol. 30/2, pp. 91–101.

Lundberg, K. (2011), "A systems thinking approach to environmental follow-up in a Swedish central public authority: Hindrances and possibilities for learning from experience", *Environmental Management*, Vol. 48/1, pp. 123-133.

Lusch, R. and S. Vargo (eds.) (2006), *The Service Dominant Logic of Marketing*. M.E. Sharpe, New York.

LVM (Ministry of Transport and Communications) (2016), *Rapporteurs to Explore the Future of the Transport and Communications System*, Press Release, 9 September 2016, LVM, Helsinki, www.lvm.fi/en/-/rapporteurs-to-explore-the-future-of-the-transport-and-communications-system.

March, J.G. (1991), "Exploration and exploitation in organizational learning", *Organization Science*, Vol. 2/1, pp. 71-87.

McCann, L. (2013), "Reforming public services after the crash: The roles of framing and hoping", *Public Administration*, Vol. 91/1, pp. 5–16.

Mulgan, G. (2005), Government, knowledge and the business of policy making: The potential and limits of evidence-based policy, *Evidence and Policy: A Journal of Research, Debate and Practice*, Vol. 1/2, pp. 215-226.

Munro, E. (2011a), Munro Review of Child Protection: Final Report, UK Department of Education, London, www.gov.uk/government/uploads/system/uploads/attachment_data/file/175391/Munro-Review.pdf.

Munro, E. (2011b), *Munro Review Of Child Protection: Interim Report – the Child's Journey.* UK Department of Education, London, www.gov.uk/government/uploads/system/uploads/attachment_data/file/206993/DFE-00010-2011.pdf.

Munro, E. (2010), *Munro Review of Child Protection: Part 1 – A Systems Analysis.* UK Department of Education, London, www.gov.uk/government/uploads/system/uploads/attachment_data/file/175407/TheMunroReview-Part_one.pdf.

Munro, E.R. and C. Lushey (2012), The impact of more flexible assessment practices in response to the Munro Review of Child Protection: Emerging findings from the trials. UK Department of Education, London, www.gov.uk/government/uploads/system/uploads/attachment_data/file/181503/CWRC-00088-2012.pdf.

National Accounting Office (NAO) (2006), *Achieving Innovation in Central Government Organizations.* National Accounting Office, London.

OECD (2017), *Embracing Innovation in Government – Global Trends 2017,* OECD, Paris, www.oecd.org/gov/innovative-government/embracing-innovation-in-government.pdf.

OECD (2016), "World Government Summit: Call for Public Innovations, Observatory of Public Information", OECD, Paris, www.oecd.org/governance/observatory-public-sector-innovation/blog/page/worldgovernmentsummitcallforpublicinnovations.htm.

OECD (2015), "Systems Innovation: Synthesis Report", OECD, Paris, www.innovationpolicyplatform.org/system-innovation-oecd-project.

Osborne, S.P. and L. Brown (2011), "Innovation, public policy and public services delivery in the UK: The word that would be king?", *Public Administration*, Vol. 89, pp. 1335-1350.

Osborne, S.P., Z. Radnor and G. Nasi (2013), "A new theory for public service management? Toward a (public) service-dominant approach", *American Review of Public Administration*, Vol. 43/2, pp. 135-158.

Overman, S. and S. Van Thiel (2016), "Agencification and Public Sector Performance: A systematic comparison in 20 countries", *Public Management Review*, Vol. 18/4, pp. 611-635.

Pärna, O and N. von Tunzelman (2007), "Innovation in the public sector: Key features influencing the development and implementation of technologically innovative public sector services in the UK, Denmark, Finland and Estonia", *Information Polity*, Vol. 12, pp. 109-125.

Pepper, M., A. Sense and K. Speare (2016), "Systems pluralism in infrastructure decision-making for socially connected greenfield communities", *Systemic Practice and Action Research*, Vol. 29/2, pp. 129-148.

Peters, B.G., J. Pierre and D.S. King (2005), "The politics of path dependency: Political conflict in historical institutionalism", *The Journal of Politics*, Vol. 67/4, pp. 1275-1300.

Pilli-Sihvola, E. et al. (2015), "Robots on land, in water and in the air. Promoting intelligent automation in transport services", *Publications of the Ministry of Transport and Communications*, 14/2015.

Potts, J. and T. Kastelle (2010), "Public sector innovation research: what's next?", *Innov.: Manage. Policy Pract.*, Vol. 12, 122-137.

Powell, M. et al. (2010), "Broadening the focus of public service consumerism", *Public Management Review*, Vol. 12, pp. 323-340.

Rittel, H.W. and M.M. Webber (1973), "Dilemmas in a general theory of planning", *Policy Sciences*, Vol. 4/2, pp. 155-169.

Scottish Government (2016), *Scotland's National Performance Framework (NPF)*, slides, June 2016, www.gov.scot/Resource/0049/00497339.pdf.

Seddon, J. (2008), Systems thinking in the public sector: The failure of the reform regime... and a manifesto for a better way. Triarchy Press Limited, Axminster, UK.

Seddon, J. (2003), *Freedom from Command and Control*. Vanguard Press, Buckingham, UK.

Snowden, D.J. and M.E. Boone (2007), "A leader's framework for decision making", *Harvard Business Review*, Vol. 85/11, p. 68.

Stanhope, V. and K. Dunn (2011), "The curious case of Housing First: The limits of evidence based policy", *International Journal of Law and Psychiatry*, Vol. 34/4, pp. 275-282.

Torugsa, N. and A. Arundel (2015), The nature and incidence of workgroup innovation in the Australian public sector: Evidence from the 2011 State of the Service survey", *Australian Journal of Public Administration*, Vol. 75, pp. 202-221.

Turner, V. (1997), *The Ritual Process*. Cornell University Press, Ithaca, NY.

van Acker, W. and Bouckaert, G. (2015), *Mapping and Analysing the Recommendations of Ombudsmen, Audit Offices and Emerging Accountability Mechanisms*, LIPSE: Learning from Innovation in Public Sector Environments (Work Package 3), European Policy Brief, LIPSE, Brussels, www.lipse.org/upload/publications/LIPSE%20WP3%20Policy%20Brief_20150324_ENG.pdf.

Verma, A. (2012), Skills for competitiveness: Country report for Canada. *OECD Local Economic and Employment Development (LEED) Working Papers*, 3, pp. 1-84.

Vittersø, G. and T. Tangeland (2015), "The role of consumers in transitions towards sustainable food consumption: The case of organic food in Norway", *Journal of Cleaner Production*, 92, pp. 91-99.

Walker, R.M. (2013), "Internal and external antecedents of process innovation: A review and extension", *Public Management Review*, 16, pp. 21-44.

Wauters, B. and M. Drinkgreve (2016), Improving the Quality of Public Service and Reducing Costs: Lessons from the Youth Protection Agency of Amsterdam

(Netherlands). Case study. Mortsel, Belgium, www.latitudeconsulting.eu/images/childprotect.docx.

WHO (2009), Systems Thinking for Health Systems Strengthening. WHO Press, Geneva.

Further reading

Arundel, A. and D. Huber (2013), "From too little to too much innovation? Issues in monitoring innovation in the public sector", *Structural Change and Economic Dynamics*, Vol. 27, pp. 146-149.

Bergen, P. and A. Reynolds (2005), "Blowback revisited: Today's Insurgents in Iraq Are tomorrow's terrorists", *Foreign Affairs*, Vol. 84, p. 2.

Betts, J. and R. Holden (2003), "Organisational learning in a public sector organisation: A case study of muddled thinking", *Journal of Workplace Learning*, Vol. 15, pp. 280-287.

Bloch, C. and M.M. Bugge (2013), "Public sector innovation – from theory to measurement. *Structural change and economic dynamics*", Vol. 27, pp. 133-145.

Jackson, M.C. et al. (2008), "Evaluating systems thinking in housing", *Journal of the Operational Research Society*, Vol. 59/2, pp. 186-197.

OECD (2011), "Innovation in Public Service Delivery: Context, Solutions and Challenges", OECD, Paris.

ODPM (Office of the Deputy Prime Minister) (2005), A Systematic Approach to Service Improvement Evaluating Systems Thinking in Housing. ODPM Publications, London.

Seadon, J.K. (2010), "Sustainable waste management systems", *Journal of Cleaner Production*, Vol. 18/16, pp. 1639-1651.

Vargo, S.L. and R.F. Lusch (2008), "Service-dominant logic: Continuing the evolution", *Journal of the Academy of Marketing Science*, Vol. 36/1, pp. 1-10.

Vargo, S.L. and R.F. Lusch (2004), "Evolving to a new dominant logic for marketing", *Journal of Marketing*, Vol. 68/1, pp. 1-17.

Chapter 2.

Towards a framework for systems transformation

This chapter starts by highlighting the multi-method nature of new systems-based practices. It discusses how systems thinking differs and complements design thinking, and how design can be used in systemic change processes. It discusses how, under conditions of complexity and uncertainty, governments can reflect in action and work with relative precision. The chapter discusses how decision makers and public services managers can consider the kinds of challenges they face, the resources available to them and what they can expect while engaging in a rigorous problem-solving process using systems approaches. Following this discussion, the chapter identifies some key principles and tactics – people and place, dwelling, connecting, framing, designing, prototyping, stewarding and evaluating – involved in using systems approaches in the public sector. Specific practices are dependent on the context, institutional capacity, problem, timeframe and resources available to public administrations as they embark on systems change.

New systems-based practices

Innovative approaches to problem solving and service delivery are proliferating across governments that are contending with complex problems for which there are few precedents or solutions. Front-line public servants are simultaneously dealing with "customers" who have come to expect tailored, responsive products and services similar to those they routinely experience in their interactions with business, especially the tech industry.

The inability of command and control systems to cope with these demands has created a vacuum into which new systems-based practices are stepping. However, many of these efforts remain at the margins, often organised into "labs" that have the space and mandate to innovate government processes. They have yet to move toward the centre of government or to tackle the norms and standards that dictate the behaviour of civil servants. The following include notable efforts to promote systems-based practices:

- In the United Kingdom, NESTA has worked to build an ecosystem of systems and design-based practices around government through its social innovation programmes, i-teams and Creative Councils, among others. The Centre for Aging Better also promotes systems-based practice (see Box 1.3).

- SITRA's Helsinki Design Lab, Strategy Unit and partnerships with organisations such as Demos Helsinki have deployed systems approaches on issues such as clean tech and urban decarbonisation. They have also worked to develop the theoretical and practical underpinnings of systems approaches and strategic design.

- The MaRS Discovery District in Toronto hosts organisations and businesses with the potential to be change agents, and helps to build their capacity and expertise. The MaRS Solutions Lab works at the intersection of design and systems thinking to develop solutions, policy and capacity around complex societal challenges such as health, work and food. Their *Periodic Table for Systems Change* (see Figure 3.14 in Chapter 3) provides a useful framework for understanding the different kinds of elements required to navigate and alter complex systems.

- In the United States, the Office of Personnel Management's Lab@OPM works to disseminate design and systems-based practices and tools across government through training programmes for government workers and contractors. It also provides a platform to bring together other federal agencies to address complex challenges.

- MindLab, Denmark's cross-government innovation group, emphasises the importance of citizen involvement, voice and co-creation, all of which necessitate systems approaches. Its staff includes designers, sociologists, ethnographers and other professionals who work in blended teams together with citizens.

- The Australian Centre for Social Innovation (TACSI), a not-for-profit funded by government, applies design and social research to co-creative processes in order to tackle difficult social, economic and environmental problems. They search for ways to crack "open the current system at crisis points" (Puttick, Baeck and Colligan, 2014) and develop new services to fulfil unmet or neglected needs. Their well-known "Family by Family" project is a good example of this approach. By working to address the seemingly intractable problem of dysfunctional families, TACSI aims to reduce the growing demands on social services by pairing families that have overcome crises with families currently in the midst of crisis. Their critical insight was not to ask how to mitigate chronic stress, but to imagine what might a successful family under difficult circumstances look like. Once they had established that the target was thriving families, not mitigation, they were able to design better, more impactful services.

Systems thinking and design thinking: different but complementary approaches

There is currently a surge of interest in *design thinking* in the public sector, especially in relation to co-designing public services with citizens through participatory processes.[1] (The proliferation of "sticky notes" in government offices is a strong sign of this shift – see the section in this chapter on *People and place*). However, the interlinkages between service design and systems thinking have to be made clear, especially as regards the emergence of "design thinking" (Rowe, 1987) and design management (e.g. see Cooper Junginger and Lockwood, 2009). The former denotes the use of design methods to match consumer needs and value, taking into consideration technological viability and business strategy (see Brown, 2008; Martin, 2009), while design management is geared more towards prototyping, although some approaches also include elements from systems thinking (e.g. understanding user experiences, ideation, rapid prototyping and systems visualisation) (Mulgan, 2014).

The increased popularity of "design thinking" in the policy realm has led to the proliferation of different toolboxes and guides on how to use design and design thinking in the public sector, some of which mention systems thinking in combination with design tools.[2] In general, these methodologies try to rationalise change processes within the public sector and are therefore reductionist to a degree. (By definition, tools and toolkits that are divorced from the underlying principles used to create them constitute a reductionist approach even when labelled "systemic".) There is friction between the context-specific nature of systems analysis and the latest push for a generic "toolbox" approach in the public sector. Nevertheless, designers working in the public sector also see themselves as craftsmen, designing for contextual demands and user needs in practice, and not for archetypical situations.

However, there are no clear-cut guidelines as to how systems thinking and design thinking approaches fit together. Some publications regard system thinking as a part of a larger design skill-set (Mulgan, 2014), while others apply design as a tool within a larger systems thinking approach (e.g. see Gharajedaghi, 2011). The origins of systems thinking and design thinking are clearly different – design thinking originated from product design approaches[3] and design emerged more broadly from architecture and product design – however, they are interlinked concepts. Systems thinkers were already using design as a concept in the 1980s, albeit largely as a "problem-solving tool" (e.g. Ackoff 1981; Argyris and Schön, 1978). What is important to note is that *systems thinking is not just systematic design*. Systems thinking at its core is oriented towards organisational learning – reflection in action. However, the practical application of systems thinking is often characterised by a narrow focus on systematic design (Li, 2002: 387).

Design is a useful bridge for integrating systems thinking into everyday organisational learning (ibid.: 392). Hence, some view the popular combination of design thinking with evidence-based policy making as a means to rejuvenate interest in systems thinking in the public sector (Wastell, 2010). However, design thinking tends to deal with events, problems and the application of tools. It concentrates on action, prototyping ("thinking through doing") and is usually associated with Herbert Simon's rational-technical problem-solving logic (Dorst and Royakkers, 2006). In many cases, the feedback loop from an implementation phase is weak (which represents a clear break from traditional design practices). Furthermore, rational problem solving may not account for more complex changes in value distribution. This is particularly notable in cases where policy makers select a solution that is unsatisfactory overall but satisfies current conditions (ibid.), potentially resulting in piecemeal solutions that hide underlying structural policy problems. Accordingly, service designers that concentrate on second or third-order design problems directly connected to user needs may neglect fourth-order design problems[4] – systems integration – which are often linked to wicked problems (Junginger, 2014: 148-149).

For example, design methodologies employed by public sector innovation labs often use rapid prototyping; however, many of these solutions do not fit within the broader public service system (Tõnurist, Kattel and Lember, 2015). This makes it difficult to move beyond experimentation to long-term exploration.[5] A systemic design guide published by Alberta CoLab exemplifies this approach (Box 2.1). While Alberta CoLab use many systems thinking tools, they do not tackle implementation, which in the public policy context may constitute the most difficult part of the process due to feedback from traditional institutions, established bureaucratic procedures and short political lifecycles.

Box 2.1. CoLab's systemic design field guide (Canada)

In 2016, Alberta CoLab published the guide *Follow the Rabbit: A Field Guide to Systemic Design*. It was developed with staff of the Government of Alberta in mind, but can be applied to different public policy areas, sectors and intersections.

CoLab outlined five key characteristics of systemic designers – they are inquiring, open, integrative, collaborative and centred. Accordingly, they adopted a simple formula: playfulness + discipline = creativity.

The guide describes a systemic design project, introducing the following phases for systems design projects: planning, workshops and evaluation. The methods used include steps such as "look" (which includes tools such as interviewing for empathy, empathy maps, keep asking why and ethnography); "frame" (rich pictures, systems maps, iceberg diagrams, CLDs, concept maps, six thinking hats, speed dating, affinity diagrams, card sorts and world cafes); "generate" (participatory prototyping and dotmocracy) and "adapt" (reflection and action space).

According to the guide, the nature of the problem should be outlined during the planning phase. A systemic design approach should be used only if the problem is complex, otherwise, such an approach would be deemed "overkill". Additional important questions to consider include: Is the client open to change? Does the client have "top cover" (i.e. a senior-level champion)? Is the client committed (i.e. has adequate resources and willing to implement the project)? And, most critically: Has the client been identified?

"Sequencing" plays an important role during project workshops and involves: bringing in external perspectives, ideation, testing, integrating findings, evaluating processes, implementing and sharing results, and maintaining momentum during workshops. Certain specific roles need to be allocated including a facilitator (usually an outside designer), recorder, note taker and narrator. Each workshop is followed by an evaluation and, after a few months, a "check back" to take note of any progress or changes. The approach is design centred and focuses on workshops, but does not explore implementation.

Systems thinking helps to place a managerial problem into context as a part of systems events (e.g. a discrete client-service interaction), and patterns and structures (rather than events alone for which design solutions are applied).[6] At the same time, systems thinking can over-emphasise analysis ("thinking it through") and neglect action, which may result in problems. In practice, the two approaches are complementary. The danger is that both approaches tend to become overly rigid when applying their specific methodologies, which can limit their use in broader policy-making circles.

Design has always been concerned with the interactions between people and things. For much of its history, these things have tended to be objects. But, increasingly, design is working at the intersection of people, processes and outcomes, making it particularly relevant for managing a transition towards human-centred policies and services. Human-centred design (HCD), strategic design, design thinking and other variations have gained traction in many administrations that are moving to re-orient processes around their citizens. Other systems approaches are also well positioned to better incorporate citizens' interests into public services as principal stakeholders.

Strategies to manage complexity: What are the options for the public sector?

Complexity arises when systems are not configured to respond to the challenges they face. Ashby's law states that any control system must be at least as complex as the system it is controlling, otherwise a complexity gap will arise from the mismatch.[7] For example, in a tax regime where legislators create increasingly complex regulations, constituents will always be able to develop more means of evading taxes than regulators can address. This situation results from the variety and quantity of avoidance schemes available to lawyers, accountants and tax advisors, which are then multiplied by the variety of individual circumstances. The solution to this complexity gap is not to make tax policy more complex, but to reduce the variety of options available to the public by simplifying the tax regime (Casti, 2012: 56). In essence, reduced variety on the regulatory side will result in a reduced number of responses on the part of those being regulated. Ashby's law may be the most important principle to consider when working on – and especially developing interventions for – complex systems.

Complexity scholars Max Boisot and Bill McKelvey have revived Ashby's law and applied it to the contemporary debate around managing organisations in increasingly complex environments. Their Law of Requisite Complexity holds that "to be efficaciously adaptive, the internal complexity of a system must match the external complexity it confronts" (McKelvey and Boisot, 2009). With respect to managing complexity, organisations have two principal adaptation strategies. The first is to simplify or reduce the complexity of incoming stimuli so as to minimise internal complexity. Such *complexity reduction* can be achieved through abstraction – for example, by creating theoretical models that make information more manageable or actionable. There are risks associated with this strategy that stem from oversimplification, such as in the banking sector where securitisation of residential mortgages shielded unaccounted risks, leading to the global financial crisis. Examples from the public sector abound, but at a systemic level, the organisation of domain authority into ministries is a form of simplification or complexity reduction. For instance, the housing sector is responsible for a significant portion of energy consumption, and people's behaviours within this context drive energy usage, yet governments have formed separate departments of housing, energy and human services. This artificial segmentation of problem spaces reduces complexity, but also limits the degree to which any single organisation can understand and take action to address systemic challenges. This results in a complexity gap between problems such as climate change and the government's ability to address these challenges holistically.

The second strategy is *complexity absorption* whereby organisations create internal complexity that is determined to be equal or greater than the external complexity it faces. Complexity absorption leads to requisite variety which in the best case permits an organisation to be adaptive, opening up new kinds of strategic options (Hämäläinen, 2015). But there are risks too: resources can be quickly depleted as the organisation grows in size or diversity (Boisot and McKelvey, 2011) and possibly becomes too complex to be effectively managed (e.g. multinational financial institutions). In the public sector, complexity absorption results in the proliferation of new internal agencies within departments or ministries. For instance, the US Department of State has as many as 71 internal Offices and Bureaus, each with its own remit, leadership, resourcing, cultural norms and legacies. This leads to the remarkable cultural phenomenon that physical proximity to the Secretary of State's office is indicative of the importance, priority or power of a Bureau or Office, as opposed to a more fluid resourcing scheme based on global affairs. On a much smaller scale, the push toward data capture and analytics is also a form of complexity absorption, as public administrations deploy tools that can potentially help them understand their environment more holistically. However, the persistent challenge of big data is the ability to understand and take action on vast amounts of new information; complexity begets complexity.

Boisot and McKelvey describe these interrelated strategies of complexity reduction and complexity absorption, and the trade-offs inherent between them, as the *Ashby Space* (ibid.). Figure 2.1 illustrates this conceptual framework and the potential of design and other systems approaches to manage complexity. The diagonal line represents requisite variety, or an ideal state of dynamic equilibrium where the variety of an organisation's responses (internal complexity) matches the incoming stimuli (external complexity). According to Ashby, equilibrium can be achieved through forms of regulation (Ashby, 1956).

It follows then that *regulation* is the key task of organisations operating in complex environments. The objective of regulation is to move toward requisite variety as complexity increases. As Boisot and McKelvey point out, "the variety that the system then has to respond to depends in part on its internal schema development and transmission capacities and in part on the operation of tuneable filters, controlled by the system's cognitive apparatus, and used by the system to separate out regularities from noise" (Boisot and McKelvey, 2011: 284).

Figure 2.1. The Ashby Space

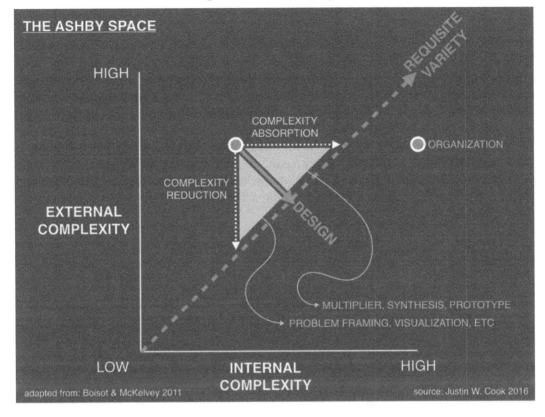

Source: Based on Boisot and McKelvey (2011).

The organisation depicted in Figure 2.2 is experiencing high levels of external complexity and facing a need for regulation to move it toward requisite variety (stability). As discussed above, there are two strategies to move toward stability within the Ashby Space: become more complex internally or reduce complexity by simplifying variety. An alternate complexity reduction strategy could be to retreat and focus only on core competencies, but this is unusual among most organisations not facing crisis and may be altogether impossible due to the interconnectedness of today's challenges.

However, a third strategy exists for working toward requisite variety that can achieve a more stable position than either complexity absorption or complexity reduction on their own. Design processes and some systems approaches are very effective tools for managing complexity and generating productive outcomes. Employing design principles and methodologies enables an organisation to transit the Ashby Space more efficiently toward requisite variety. The field's growing adoption across multiple sectors where normative tools are no longer achieving results is indicative of its success. While design methodologies still remain largely marginal to more firmly established strategy processes, a shift is underway that is pushing designers deep into organisations and making them part of the system itself. This is enabling designers to move beyond "innovation" teams responsible for novelty to participants engaged in implementation and, therefore, the evolution of the system itself. This shift provides designers with the opportunity to engage self-adaptive systems directly (Ito, 2016).

Design has traditionally worked to make sense of complexity through problem framing, visualisation, ethnographic practices, working with relative precision and across disciplinary cultures, and so on. These methodologies do not artificially simplify complexity, but aim to contextualise and order information and then make it actionable. Crucially, design processes that include implementation also create a feedback loop between information, ideas, people and action through prototyping and iteration. Rather than loading more complexity into the structure of an organisation (complexity absorption), design allows for variety to be explored and exploited (and thus reduced) *within the process itself.* By optimising reduction and absorption strategies, design and systems approaches transit the Ashby Space more productively towards requisite variety, enabling what Boisot and McKelvey term the *complex regime* (Figure 2.2), where complexity can be embraced and successful schema can be developed. The following sections explore in greater detail systems approaches and design methodologies that have proven effective within the Ashby Space.

Figure 2.2. Three complexity regimes

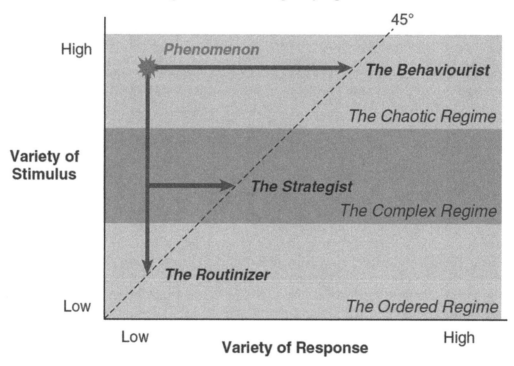

Source: Boisot and McKelvey (2011).

Returning to the question of systems change in crisis versus static conditions, what can be learned from the Ashby Space framework? In the face of crisis, organisations tend to adopt a complexity reduction strategy in order to make a situation manageable. This is understandable, and in some cases appropriate. However, experience shows that this approach carries significant risks associated with decisions that can worsen outcomes. For instance, in the aftermath of Hurricane Katrina, which devastated New Orleans in 2005, the Federal Emergency Management Agency (FEMA) supplied thousands of what came to be known as FEMA Trailers, mobile units intended to provide temporary housing. While this quick reaction provided housing relief for those who had lost their homes, many of the trailers contained dangerous levels of formaldehyde, which caused significant health issues. Worse still, as of 2015 – a decade after the crisis – people continue to occupy FEMA trailers (Smith, 2015), suggesting an inherent conflict or error in what was designed to be a short-term solution. However, alternative examples of progressive, productive reactions to crisis also exist. As Helsinki Design Lab explored in their 2013 case study *Rebuilding Constitución*, the response to the devastating tsunami that destroyed the city of Constitución, Chile, shows that a systemic, inclusive, co-created solution to redesigning and rebuilding an entire city can be done both efficiently and successfully (Boyer, Cook and Steinberg 2013: 25).

Under static conditions, both complexity absorption and complexity reduction can occur. Returning to the example of the US State Department, the proliferation of Bureaus and Offices suggests a high level of complexity absorption for an administrative body charged with managing global affairs for the US Government. However, just as departmentalisation of large segments of public sector problem spaces is a form of complexity reduction, the same holds true for the internal structure of a single department or ministry. When conditions are fairly static (e.g. the absence of a large-scale conflict such as the Second World War or the rise of polarising adversaries during the Cold War), organisations like the State Department find themselves attempting to both reduce and absorb complexity, which moves them no closer to requisite variety. The key question in a static condition is: How does an organisation create an opportunity to transit the Ashby space toward requisite variety when there is no external stimulus to force action?

Working with relative precision

For many in the public sector, the fiduciary responsibilities that come with public office require a conservative approach to risk: with authority comes responsibility. This responsibility can be realised either through strict regulations on policy design and implementation, or tacitly through behavioural norms within institutions. In most areas, precision and certainty of evidence are understood to be a fundamental precursor to decision making. This is especially true for domains such as health care and education where the public expect positive outcomes, not experimentation and risk of failure. While it is certain that governments use evidence in their decision making, it is unclear whether the evidence fully informs policy or whether decision makers are able to comprehend evidence due to time, expertise, complexity or other constraints. The capture, analysis and transmission of evidence can also be a very time-consuming process. Political cycles and research cycles operate by very different clock speeds. Policy problems, especially certain social or environmental challenges, can be resistant to the formulation of comparable data. Moreover, evidence itself can be politicised – accepted by some as science and derided by others as fiction. These factors lead to a conflicted state: on the one hand, evidence is necessary; on the other, evidence may not be useful in a decision-making process.[8]

Enter then, wicked problems. As discussed above, wicked problems are emergent, meaning that they result from the interaction of smaller subsystems. Typically, science and evidence creation are most effective and precise at the level of the subsystem. For instance, the cognitive development of children can be well explained by neuroscience and psychology, but it is difficult to understand how learning emerges from the confluence of social, cultural, economic, environmental and biological factors. The problem that should concern policy makers the most – in this example, learning – is out of reach of the more narrowly defined domains of scientific inquiry. While some have begun calling for a second-order science approach to policy making, much work must be done to develop the field before it can be widely applied (see Hodgson and Leicester, 2016).

So, what can be done when facing a problem with no "definitive definition"? For designers and systems thinkers, the answer lies in their ability to work with relative precision. To overcome barriers stemming from uncertainty, it is necessary to comparatively appraise knowledge about a wicked problem. In practice, this means treating qualitative and quantitative data with equal rigour and by actively searching for – or inventing bridges between – the two. This process usually requires intuition and testing. The former, while perhaps an uncomfortable topic for many disciplines because of its apparent lack of seriousness, is in actuality a critical skill honed by experience and central to many designers' practice. In the context of strategy, intuition requires full investment of time and thought, so as to acquire a sense about how things fit together (Boyer, Cook and Steinberg 2011: 37). The latter, testing, is also dependent on intuition to the extent that it requires experience to know how to test ideas efficiently and productively.

Visualisation is also an effective tool for working with relative precision. In its most common form, visualisation is a sketch. Sketching allows the rapid transposition of ideas to paper, recording concepts while still allowing for addition, subtraction and interpretation. Precision can be increased or decreased in several ways. For instance, Figure 2.3 shows a collection of Picasso's famous "Bull" lithographs. On the left, he begins with fully developed drawings based upon a visually accurate portrait of a bull. On the right are rapid sketches that distil the essence of the bull to a few lines. Each lithograph effectively communicates the idea of a bull, but some allow for more interpretation than others. This interpretative space serves a purpose when confronting wicked problems. It allows for differing perspectives to enter a representation of an idea or analysis without relying on narrative, which itself can become so complex and circular so as to be disabling. Sketches and other forms of visualisation also preserve ideas so that they may be easily returned to over the course of work. Words on the other hand, unless carefully recorded, can be fleeting and lost during the process. Narrative can be difficult to re-contextualise, as anyone who has thought, "that seemed like such a good idea at the time" can attest.

Figure 2.3. Picasso's "Bull" lithographs, 1945

Source: Picasso www.flickr.com/photos/sorarium/8578925321.

Working with relative precision also allows designers to propose solutions before all the facts are known. This pre-factual process is familiar to the practice of architecture, where designs for whole or parts of buildings, landscapes, infrastructures and so on are proposed well in advance of having fundamental information such as budget, location, occupancy and other constraints. In other disciplines, such as engineering, it is critical to have the most complete information possible before developing a solution in order to manage the risk of failure. This approach is productive when variables are known, but virtually impossible when working with wicked problems.

A pre-factual process enables an *open-ended solution* to be developed yielding at least two principal benefits. First, developing a solution early in the process creates a test case based in part on the unique problem being tackled rather than a generic theory. From this early prototype, greater understanding of the problem itself may be assembled. Second, because a solution was developed early and with the expectation that it will change, it can evolve radically as more information is gathered. Ideally, this results in solutions that are more robust and better tailored to their specific context.

Toward a systems transformation process

This section outlines a systems transformation process and draws on the authors' experience and case study research. Each subsection outlines in general terms the key elements of success. Greater specificity is highly dependent on the context, institutional capacity, problem, timeframe and resources available to public administrations as they embark on systems change. As discussed above, each wicked problem is essentially unique, which prohibits many one-to one comparisons between systems tactics. However, strategy and principles should be transferrable despite the contextual variance inherent in large-scale systems. Where possible, the report provides examples from the public sector to help illustrate how these principles can be applied. As these are necessarily short, please refer to the case studies in Chapter 3 for further analysis.

People and place

While the value of having good people working in supportive spaces may seem obvious, it is frequently overlooked as an indulgence, especially in the public sector. Yet these two variables – talent and workspace – are among the most important considerations of any highly successful start-up or established, innovative company. The same is true when applying systems approaches to complex problems.

Design is an inherently optimistic act and systems transformation in the public sector is ultimately concerned with improving people's lives. As such, it is critical to have a core team in place that is invested in both the change *and* betterment of a system.

The selection of individuals into teams should be done carefully. Having lateral thinkers and multiple disciplines present is important, but not as critical as their ability to maintain applied optimism. Systems change can be a slow, grinding process. Possessing optimism in the value and purpose of change helps to bridge the countervailing forces certain to emerge. That said, design and systems thinking rarely succeed with standard collaborative processes that can be completed during one-hour meeting slots. This is because wicked problems cannot be solved by a single discipline creating an optimum solution based on its tools and worldview. Multiple arenas of deep knowledge must be integrated, even when these seem contradictory. This synthesis across disciplines is possible when teams are able and willing to work inter-methodologically in an effort to find the best process fit for the topic at hand. Moreover, loose fits are common under uncertain conditions, but should not be feared or forced into greater conformity.

It is also useful to embed external expertise within a team for a fixed period. For instance, the Collaboratory at the US Department of State contracted a designer trained at the Rhode Island School of Design, in order to bring a new set of skills to help build out a new platform for collaboration. Similarly, members of the Strategy Unit at the Finnish Innovation Fund (SITRA) have joined the Prime Minister's Office and the Ministry of Economic Affairs and Employment for fixed terms to both introduce new ways of working and thinking into government, but also to improve SITRA's intelligence about how government operates. These "exchange programmes" help to expand ways of working and cultural norms and provide a space for new practices to emerge.

It must be recognised at the outset that, for some, systems transformation might equal loss, including employment, seniority or job satisfaction. Those that stand to lose should not be excluded, however, as they undoubtedly possess deep insights into the machinery of systems. In practice, this can translate into engaging those that stand to lose in a carefully managed process that allows them to redesign their roles within the new system.

Place is also important as it signifies the investment an institution is making in the process. Working in an isolated basement versus a public space closely connected to the heart of an organisation, or even a storefront rented in the city, sends two very different messages to those involved, including external stakeholders. Even when space is at a premium, seeing to their psychological and physical comforts can provide teams with a baseline sense of wellbeing that will help them overcome obstacles such as the frustration that is a normal by-product of ambiguity. It can be simple: remarkable effects can be realised when managers provide employees with access to decent coffee and good food. Google, Facebook and other companies learned this to their benefit long ago.

Working spaces must also enable dedicated, long-term collaboration. Given the complexity of systems approaches, it is not reasonable to expect to hold all relevant critical information in one's mind at all times. Pinning visualisations, artefacts, reports, images and so on to the walls of a workspace can spur new, connective thinking as a project unfolds.

Dwelling

Wicked problems often outstrip the ability to define them effectively. This mismatch between problem and definition sometimes arises from old concepts that have not been updated or recast to meet a changed landscape.

For instance, *civics* is a concept and practice central to the American understanding of a citizen's duties to the state. Today, civics is widely understood to be satisfied by voting. But in the past, the civic lives of Americans were much richer, connecting individuals to communities and communities to government. A search of the vast Google Books library using the Google NGram Viewer, which highlights the frequency in usage of words, shows that the term "civics" was actively used in the first half of the twentieth century, but began a precipitous decline in the 1960s. Since that time, the word appears at a much lower frequency, even after 9/11. This suggests that the idea of civics, which was once a foundational concept, has not been renewed for half a century. Meanwhile, technology, identity politics and structural changes have pushed Americans away from their government and one another.

The term "dwelling" means investing time to understand and articulate both the problem and the objective. Even in the context of discrete problems, it is easy to include significant biases or overly rely on tacit knowledge. To unpack the tacit dimensions of understanding and minimise bias, it is important to ensure that topics are sufficiently explored and that related issues are given more than a passing glance. This is especially true when working with complexity where some causal factors may not even be directly observable. Accounting for all sources of input, including those that are unspoken, may help reveal a more complete problem architecture.

Systems change and especially design processes often begin with a conversation about purpose. Defining the purpose of something helps to understand why it should exist and how best to achieve this aim. But for many central public institutions or constructs, purpose has gone undefined for decades. Take education for instance. When was the last time a country had a society-wide conversation about why and to what end it educates its children? Similarly, what is the purpose of health care: is it to extend life or improve wellbeing? Such questions cannot be answered without a debate on purpose. Time assigned to dwelling encourages this kind of searching and thinking. In a public sector context, using the term "dwelling" may generate alarm. Other phrases adapted from project management such as "phase zero" can be useful here.

In the language and practice of design, dwelling is often described as divergence or exploration. This phase is then followed by subsequent phases that consist of defining what has been learned, or convergence. The UK Design Council's famous *Double Diamond* diagram captures this notion well (Figure 2.4).

Figure 2.4. Double Diamond

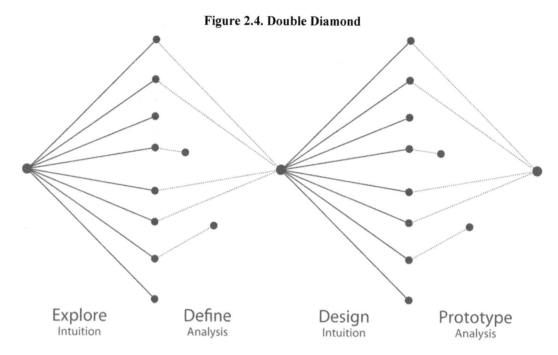

Sources: Adapted from Helsinki Design Lab (2010) and UK Design Council.

Dwelling also suggests that alternate means of coping with information may be required. For example, storytelling, when combined with harder quantitative data, can be an effective tool for understanding complex systems. But to design an effective story, phenomena may have to be observed and analysed through multiple lenses. Models may have to be built to illuminate relationships and expose gaps. This takes time and resources and the willingness to dedicate them to an area of work that may not produce timely or obvious results. In this context, dwelling acts as a form of due diligence for complex systems that will pay dividends in later stages by accelerating the ability to make meaningful propositions.

In a public sector context, dwelling can be enabled through engagement processes where officials interact with citizens and other stakeholders to understand their lived experience (see the next section). The key is to spend time to align what is learned in the field with what are understood to be the limits and opportunities present in a system, in relation to a given problem. For instance, if an administration is interested in developing better services for aging populations, gathering more data from constituents will not be sufficient. These data must be made actionable by developing new principles, frameworks or logics from which interventions can be designed. Making information actionable requires the ability and resources to be *reflective* – another term for dwelling.

Connecting

To understand citizens, it is essential to get close to them; to see their lives, their desires, their fears and their successes through their lived experience. This action of *connecting* is itself extremely difficult, especially for governments, where institutional structures often thwart the ability to develop a holistic understanding of people and the issues they face. In order to connect, engagements with citizens must be meaningful, generative and respectful, and should not take the form of arms-length instruments such as surveys.[9] Connecting takes time and resources and makes use of tools such as videography that may not be readily available or familiar. Working with citizens in co-creative processes can be unpredictable and yield results contrary to an administration's perception of acceptable or desirable practice. Careful facilitation is also required. In the best cases, good facilitation destabilises authority and expertise, allowing controversial issues to be explored and captured more completely as citizens feel free to challenge political and business interests.[10]

The kind of knowledge generated by connecting with people is perhaps equally challenging, as it does not enjoy the same universality as quantitative knowledge. Centuries of parsing economic data has led to their extensive use in driving decision making. But what about less structured, qualitative data? The difficulties involved for decision makers in confronting a narrative, having strategic conversations, and then reaching unbiased decisions about policy and services, lead almost inevitably to the traditional approach of mild, distant citizen engagement.

However, the social science ethnography provides critical capabilities that allow researchers to work with qualitative data as rigorously as quantitative data. Ethnographic practices have gained traction and, indeed, have become central within many design and systems methodologies. While it is typically modified (i.e. simplified) from its stricter tenets in the academy, "ethnography light" can still be a rigorous observational and analytic practice. A deeper examination is unfortunately beyond the scope of this report.[11] However, when considering an ethnographic approach, it is critical to bear in mind that observation is not a passive process (Simpson, 2011). As one Brown University ethnographer said, "ethnography means making the strange familiar and the familiar strange",[12] indicating that in the act of observing, it is important to recognise the implications of the observer's presence and the role interpretation and bias will play in reaching conclusions.

In connecting with citizens, it is also critical to involve a diverse representation of the public. Without diversity, even the best co-creative processes can mirror standard engagement practices, which tend to bias proximal or known stakeholders. They can and should include individuals that may not have a direct stake in the process. Their disinterest can provide useful ballast to conclusions that are too easily reached.

For public service managers, connecting can be done with a variety of tools that exist on a spectrum from low proximity to high proximity. On the low side, questionnaires mailed or sent electronically can provide basic information from those who respond. On the high side, heavily facilitated co-creation processes can engage citizens on a much deeper level, raising the possibility (and risk, if not realised) of a deep sense of ownership and commitment to the outcomes. Engaging citizens in experimentation around public policy or programmatic solutions can be a middle ground. For instance, the Prime Minister's Office in Finland has developed a digital experimentation platform for citizens, following the outcome of a PMO project led by the think tank Demos Helsinki and the Finnish Environment Institute. The objective is to crowdsource useful ideas on ways to improve Finland, develop them into experimental proposals and scale the proposals if successful (see Figure 2.5 and the case study in Chapter 3) (Demos Helsinki, 2015a). This form of connecting engages citizens and gives them a sense of shared responsibility in the work and success of government.

Figure 2.5. The experimentation process

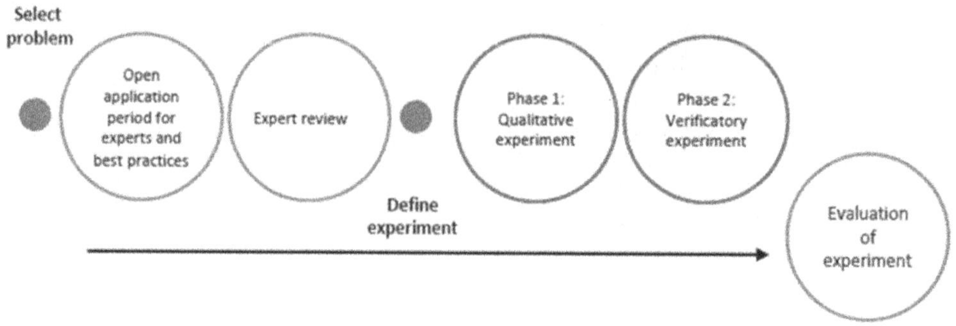

Source: Demos Helsinki (2015b).

Framing

The problem with complex, systems challenges is that it is difficult to ascertain the exact *nature* of the problem. As noted earlier, there are no definitive definitions of wicked problems. So how can the problem be identified? More specifically, how can the problem be *framed* so that action may be taken?

Framing, or in the context of design, *problem framing* is a key method designers and systems thinkers use to unpick and ultimately work around dilemmas and paradoxes that have prevented change from occurring. A problem frame stakes out the territory in which action will be taken in order to achieve a desired outcome. Consider, for instance, a physics teacher that wants her students to gain greater proficiency in core scientific principles. One framing option is to design better exercises that cover principles more comprehensively. Another is to turn students into scientists so that they can discover principles directly through inquiry. Each approach is aimed at the same objective, but depending on how the problem is framed, either curriculum or pedagogy will be the focus of the solution.

Problem frames link the desired outcome with a definition of how a solution might be organised (the patterns of relationships between parts). It leaves out the specific elements that will be deployed, as these are determined after a problem frame appears promising (Dorst, 2015: 53). Framing is a dynamic process where multiple outcomes and solutions are explored as an understanding of the problem, outcome and context evolve and are refined. However, problem frames should be formulated with some attention paid to feasibility, especially within a highly regulated environment such as a public administration. If the desired outcome and possible approaches are not aligned with the capacity of an institution or collaborative body, it can become disruptive.

Hamel and Prahalad (1999) outlined a related concept for the management community in the *Harvard Business Review*. Their concept of *strategic intent* establishes a course of action based on the available methods and a desired outcome: "the goal of Strategic Intent is to fold the future back into the present … [W]hile clear about ends, it is flexible as to means." Within organisations, strategic intent provides a shared platform on which ideas can be explored and built into solutions while maintaining focus on overall objectives. For the design community, strategic intent can be blended with other objectives such as targeting specific populations or developing durable products.

In his book *Frame Innovation*, Kees Dorst (2015) offers a useful, although demanding, nine-part "frame creation process model":

1. Archaeology: analyse the problem in depth as well as earlier attempts to solve it.

2. Paradox: investigate why the problem is hard to solve.

3. Context: explore key stakeholders of the problem and their environment, behaviours, etc.

4. Field: examine the broader landscape surrounding the problem.

5. Themes: analyse and articulate deeper factors at play in the field.

6. Frames: investigate implications of possible actions given themes and outcome.

7. Futures: "think forward" to see if the frame will lead to viable solutions.

8. Transformation: critically evaluate different solutions and their feasibility over time.

9. Integration: ensure frames and solutions can be well integrated into stakeholder organisations.

A lighter approach to problem framing is to ask a series of How Might We (HMW) questions. HMWs are a common tool used in design thinking methodologies within corporations and consultancies. The key is that the question avoids using phrases such as "how can we do this" where "can" implicates additional questions about risk, capacity or other challenges that can derail a framing process. As Tim Brown, CEO of IDEO, explained in the *Harvard Business Review*:

The "how" part assumes there are solutions out there – it provides creative confidence, "Might" says we can put ideas out there that might work or might not – either way, it's OK. And the "we" part says we're going to do it together and build on each other's ideas (Berger, 2012).

Balancing ambition and feasibility is important for HMW questions. For example, "how might we deliver more accessible digital services to seniors?" is likely to work better than "how might we improve the lives of seniors?"

Other approaches that share traits similar to framing include systems mapping and modelling, scenario planning, forecasting and design fiction, among others. The limitation of these methods is that they are biased towards what is or what should be, rather than how to get there.

Designing

Today there is no lack of vision in the world, but vision alone is hard to act on (Boyer, Cook and Steinberg, 2011).

It is impossible to give a full accounting of design, design practices and methodologies, as well as the diverse world of design cultures, within the space of a few paragraphs. However, there are a few useful concepts in the context of wicked problems and public administrations working towards better public services.

Design has two fundamental concerns: first, to order information into concepts, logics and rationales and, second, to create processes that produce useful outcomes.[13] Traditionally, this has meant working through a set of constraints provided by a client to identify an approach, develop a novel solution and then establish a fabrication process that will produce the desired outcome; say a chair or a tea cup. For a world of wicked problems, design is proving an essential tool for *specifying intentions* – a critically important capacity when it may be hard to understand what problem is actually causing the symptoms, let alone what must be done. Design has also always been operative at the intersection of intention and realisation, analysis and execution. It is a discipline constructed around the feedback loop between ideas held and actions taken. This makes it particularly well suited to function rigorously in ambiguous environments where precedents have little value.

How to begin a design process? First, see the sections above, then ask a few questions. Kees Dorst provides a simple equation (Dorst, 2015: 45) that has proven useful when facilitating teams of non-designers to solve complex problems:

WHAT + HOW = OUTCOME

Where WHAT refers to the constituent elements such as people and things, HOW refers to the patterns of relationships or connections between them. OUTCOME is the observed phenomena, the result of a process where the elements interact. In a typical deductive reasoning process where cause and effect are being determined, knowing the "what" and "how" allows the outcome to be predicted.

However, design processes change the knowns in the equation:

???? + ???? = OUTCOME

Here, something is known about the outcome (objective), but the elements and relationships are still to be determined. Dorst terms this equation "design abduction", in which "two unknowns lead to a process of creative exploration" (ibid.: 49). This concept is especially useful for complex challenges where it may only be possible to determine the desired outcome. The elements and how they fit together will then depend on a variety of other factors.

A discussion about desired outcomes is similar to defining a vision for an alternate future. In the author's experience, a positive vision for the future is a critical piece of infrastructure from which all other ideas, frameworks and solutions are hung. After framing an outcome/vision, it is important to describe the principles that will govern that alternate future. In most circumstances, the principles answer the "how" variable in Dorst's equation. For instance, when British colonists in the North American colonies created a vision for a future where government was "for the people and by the people", they also defined the principles that would guide decision making, such as a representative democracy and separation of powers. Taken together, vision and principles form the conceptual framework of a design for systems transformation process.

The next step is to determine solutions (the "what" in Dorst's equation) that can intervene in an extant system and move it towards the desired future. In an ideal scenario, a group of solutions (remember that there is no optimum solution to wicked problems) forms a portfolio that exceeds the sum of its parts because of the synergistic nature of the solutions working together on a systemic challenge. The portfolio functions as a kind of systems acupuncture.

It should be pointed out that the term *solutions* should be used carefully in the context of systems change. Solutions have neat boundaries in terms of time and scope and interact with systems in predictable ways. Interventions (the authors' preferred term) are different in that they are designed with the system in mind. They anticipate a reaction by the system and are positioned to constructively incorporate the reaction while still working toward original objectives. Fundamentally, solutions are finite, while interventions more open ended and adaptable.

Prototyping

Today, prototyping (experimenting) is a well-understood concept in the product design and technology industry. However, prototyping approaches are increasingly being used in the public sector[14] and innovation labs in higher education,[15] as well as other sectors. Prototyping involves early-stage testing of ideas, well before a final product is fully conceived. The process seeks to answer questions that cannot be uncovered through further analysis or deduction. Typically, only portions of solutions are tested to establish how an idea will perform according to certain factors. In design and construction, for instance, this often involves building a portion of a building's facade at scale on or near the site to test how it performs according to local environmental factors.

According to NESTA:

Prototyping can be applied in the same way to public services. Prototyping of public services might be a way of testing early-stage ideas with service users to help choose between alternatives. It can also be used to think through key aspects of how a service would run and test it with people. Prototyping is a flexible methodology; it can be used to develop new services or improve existing services. It can be applied to the development of simple or more complex services and, depending on the level of depth required, it can be low-cost and quick or it can be more complex and take longer (NESTA, 2011, 6).

Public sector examples of prototyping include temporary new bus routes in cities where new services are needed, but true demand cannot be reliably gauged. In person-to-person service scenarios, prototypes can test new environmental conditions, such as service centre design and barriers (or lack thereof) between citizens and front line workers. Interactions can also be prototyped through role playing to test the length, content, tone, usefulness and so on, of customer engagements. This helps bring the citizen closer to the process and ensures that public services are meaningful to them, as opposed to most efficient for the administration.

The value of a prototyping process is typically worth the additional cost, as it ultimately reduces the final risk of failure. In the context of systems change, prototyping serves another function, which is to help produce greater insights about the nature of the problem itself and to build confidence among stakeholders that impactful solutions are being developed. When engaged in work that is without precedent and where ambiguity reigns, the only way to gather evidence may be to test an idea empirically. Prototyping ultimately leads to better services that have been developed at lower risk and with the buy-in of key stakeholders (ibid.: 15-16).

It is important to remember that prototyping can be conducted without significant resources. It can be both low risk and low cost. In the public sector, experimentation budgets are rare and procurement rules can slow momentum. The best solution may be to just build and test an idea, even if the execution is imperfect. A "hacker's" ethos can help drive work forward, even when institutions prove too rigid.

On a practical note, it is also important to document evidence when prototyping. Not only does this make feedback loops more useful, it also provides evidence for current and future stakeholders about the value of an initiative. Evidence generated from prototypes can be used to gauge risks associated with scaling up or investing in further refinement, such as when deciding whether or not to proceed with a pilot phase.

Stewarding

Helsinki Design Lab describes stewardship – with respect to systems change – as "the art of getting things done amidst a complex and dynamic context. Stewardship is a core ability for agents of change when many minds are involved in conceiving a course of action, and many hands in accomplishing it" (Boyer, Cook and Steinberg, 2013: 7). Stewardship is what happens after an implementation phase begins. It is not *execution* nor is it *neutral* (ibid.: 15). It differs from many traditional project management techniques in that it opens up opportunities to change directions, both tactical and strategic, once work has begun and new information about the system or problem becomes available. The core premise of stewardship rests on the notion that solutions, in the context of wicked problems, are never optimal. Rather, solutions should be understood to be interventions into a system to which the system will react, requiring adjustment on the part of the intervention in order to achieve impact. The best public service designers work to minimise negative or unexpected system reactions, employing techniques such as human-centred design and co-creation to ensure that the system will be receptive to the intervention and that, to some degree, it is a response to demand that is either expressed or latent. But even well-designed interventions will require adjustment: stewardship collapses the gap between analysis and execution common in policy spheres.

Stewardship can also be understood as a form of agile leadership during a project phase that is often viewed as not requiring significant decision making (i.e. "we figure out what to do, then we do it"). It involves continuous calibration between evolving contextual realities and desired outcomes. It is similar to the notion of strategic intent (discussed earlier) in that *folding the future back into the present* requires a constant, robust connection between objectives, methods and systems dynamics.

This requires several modifications to traditional approaches. First, resources must be distributed differently. Typical public sector procurement approaches are aimed at ensuring that deliverables match specifications decided well before the work begins. In a command and control environment, this makes sense. But in the context of wicked or systemic problems, the outcome, by definition, cannot be predetermined. There is no "theory of change" before the project begins. The theory is based on developing an understanding of the problem and the system(s) in which the problem is situated. Resourcing therefore needs to be more carefully balanced across all project phases, ideally allowing the project team to take advantage of new opportunities as they emerge, or unsuccessful paths are closed. When working opportunistically it is of course important to pay careful attention to scope creep through active vigilance. This need not take the form of a heavy reporting regime, but a regular check is necessary to ensure that work is developing according to expectations. Architecture offices have a tradition of asking each project team to present their work at the end of each week to the whole office. This tradition not only provides the team with an opportunity to demonstrate leadership and ensure the project is meeting the office's and client's objectives, it also creates a productive, dialogic atmosphere among rank and file employees. Even physicians have a similar process called Morbidity and Mortality meetings (or M&Ms) where they discuss practices, policies, errors and successes, so as to ensure progress, despite a context defined mostly by unique transactions.

Second, authority must be distributed differently. In a typical command and control or analyse-then-execute process, decision-making authority resides in the initial scoping and resourcing decisions. Implementation in this context, by definition, should not require further decision making that exceeds the scope or initial framing. Stewardship, however, necessitates the authority to continue making decisions as the project develops. In other words, authority is distributed across all project phases, rather than being front-loaded. This is because (as explored above), the problem cannot be fully understood prior to the intervention. In fact, the problem may never succumb to full analysis if it is a wicked problem. This fundamentally challenges an approach where analysis is expected to reveal the full scope of issues to be addressed, leaving only decisions about how to address them and the necessary resources required.

Third, timelines (and therefore processes) are unpredictable and should be as open ended as possible. This is especially challenging in the public sector for a multitude of reasons, not least of which is the apparent inefficiency that open-endedness might suggest. It is much easier and acceptable to begin and complete a programme on time and on budget, even if the programme does not actually improve the situation. But systems change takes time and is unpredictable, and processes must accommodate long timeframes and the ability to adjust to meet new demands. Stewardship is the practice of managing this unpredictability.

Finally, stewardship arises naturally out of any truly collaborative process. Why? Because collaboration always carries some kind of cost that is generally a product of the mismatch between different organisational cultures, norms, policies and even professional languages. This cost introduces the possibility of needing to change directions, rethink assumptions or allocate resources differently. The adaptive approaches to resourcing, authority, timeframes and process that are present in a steward's toolkit make meaningful collaboration possible.

One example of stewardship in practice (among others) is explored in the book *Legible Practises* (Boyer, Cook and Steinberg, 2013) in the context of the United Kingdom's Government Digital Services (GDS) programme. The concept of "public beta" builds on an idea borrowed from the tech sector but applied to public services. Technology companies often release products in *beta* mode before they are considered complete. For instance, Google's Gmail platform famously operated in beta for more than five years during which time it gained more than 100 million users (Lapidos, 2009). A similar idea operates in the public sector: "make services available to the public before they are fully refined and use this beta period as a way of collecting feedback to further refine the project" (Boyer, Cook and Steinberg, 2013: 128). GOV.UK, was launched by GDS in beta mode, in order to create interest, buy-in and feedback from the public. Attaching the idea and even the label "beta" to the product signalled to the public that GOV.UK was a work in progress with a built-in process for improvement. In addition to the aspects of stewardship outlined above, a public beta period also requires a different tolerance (and system to receive feedback) for scrutiny by critics, and therefore courage on the part of public managers. As Laura Bunt notes in her NESTA blog on the topic: "beta indicates a culture of continuous improvement. Trial and error, learning and adapting – principles inherent in this stage of usability testing – are important in ensuring that services adapt to our changing needs and expectations."[16]

Evaluating

Experience suggests that evaluating systems transformation efforts can be a fraught exercise. Systems normally change over long timescales, and change in unpredictable ways. In the course of the upheaval, causalities can easily be lost. In the drive to measure impact in every facet of society, consideration should be given to propriety and the value of trying to measure what may not actually be measureable.

This is not to say that developing an evidence base is not important. Evidence is critical to many aspects of systems change work, not to mention its value in ensuring that the public interest is being served. But evaluation should be carefully designed so as to have a minimal impact on the work itself. As Christopher Wren, the architect of St. Paul's Cathedral in London placed on his epitaph in the crypt: "Reader, if you seek his monument – look around you".

In the public sector context, this might mean working with stakeholders throughout a project to co-develop a set of measures or performance metrics that are project-specific and measured during and well after an implementation/stewardship phase. This will require trust and resourcing at the outset of a project to distribute evaluation authority to project teams. It might also mean waiting for months or years after a project has been completed before gathering data. Longitudinal analysis might become the new norm for public administrations working on complex challenges. This will require new means of gathering, storing, analysing and eventually sense making. Some organisations working on issues that cross traditional government structures have started to discuss the need for systems-based and "readiness for change" metrics (see Box 2.2).

Box 2.2. The search for meaningful measurement in the Early Intervention Foundation

The United Kingdom's What Works Centre for Early Intervention[17] is exploring the typologies of components and degrees of multi-agency systems that are most effective in securing early intervention for vulnerable children and families. Although published evidence on the impact of multi-agency systems is limited, there is demand at both the national and local level to identify the elements of systems that are most effective, and to build an evidence base on which future systems can be designed and implemented.

Key issues which the Early Intervention Foundation is exploring with government and local transformation leaders include: the weakness of traditional evaluation methodologies for complex and changing systems; the need for a common set of terms and metrics to classify and compare children's systems; the importance of "readiness for change" with regard to implementation and delivery of outcomes; the need for tools to aid system design and evaluation; and the importance of national leadership, guidance and support for local systems to be more effective.

Moreover, given that evidence might be unstructured, originate from non-traditional sources or be gathered via opportunistic means, analysis tools will need to be adaptable. They will also need to have equal facility with both quantitative and qualitative data, for instance, and perhaps find expression through narrative or film as opposed to spreadsheets. But more importantly, decision makers and managers will have to exercise leadership as they work with the uncertainty inherent in this kind of ambiguous information landscape. They may face additional scrutiny as the public sector (along with other fields)[18] transitions toward better use of second and third-order evidence.

The present relationship with evidence may well become more fluid. But perhaps certainty was never as certain as believed. One only needs to think back to the global financial crisis to see the pitfalls of "evidence" and certainty. As J.L. Austin wrote in *Sense and Sensibilia* (1962):

> *The situation in which I would properly be said to have evidence for the statement that some animal is a pig is that, for example, in which the beast itself is not actually on view, but I can see plenty of pig-like marks on the ground outside its retreat. If I find a few buckets of pig-food, that's a bit more evidence, and the noises and the smell may provide better evidence still. But if the animal then emerges and stands there plainly in view, there is no longer any question of collecting evidence; its coming into view doesn't provide me with more evidence that it's a pig, I can now just see that it is.*

Notes

1   See, for example, the wealth of resources on public services available from the Design Council website: www.designcouncil.org.uk/resources/search/im_field_objective/public-services-486.

2   For example, see the materials available from: http://social-labs.com/toolkits.

3   This is largely attributed to David Kelley and IDEO Design (see Kelley and VanPatter, 2005).

4   Buchanan (2001) defines the four orders of design as symbols, things, actions and thoughts, with the corresponding design areas of graphic design, industrial design, interaction design and environmental design.

5   In the context of social innovation, see Brown and Wyatt (2010).

6   See the discussion in Dunne and Martin (2006).

7   In 1956, the cybernetician W. Ross Ashby published *An Introduction to Cybernetics* in which he described the internal order of a system as a response to the environmental or external forces it faces. His Law of Requisite Variety stated "only variety can destroy variety" (Ashby, 1956: 207), which was later rephrased by Stafford Beer as the more well-known phrase "variety absorbs variety". Both Ashby and Beer were describing a state of dynamic stability wherein systems can only control input (perturbations) to the extent that they have sufficient internal variety to react. For example, in order to make a choice between two competing alternatives A and B, the decider must be able to accept or become either A or B in order to choose one of the possibilities (see http://pespmc1.vub.ac.be/REQVAR.html).

8   See the Alliance for Useful Evidence: www.alliance4usefulevidence.org.

9   For example, the Centre for Ageing Better in the UK has worked together with diverse neighbourhoods within Greater Manchester on the complex problem of "worklessness". Each area has its own distinct demographic, geography, culture and

pre-existing assets that require consideration. Using co-design, the centre brings together local providers and residents within a space where they can openly share their views and ideas on the growing challenge.

10   See Helsinki Design Lab's (2013) writing on Hybrid Forums.

11   Ethnography has many variations including Hybrid Forums (see Callon, Lascoumes and Barthe, 2009). See also the vast sphere of co-creative processes aimed at connecting authentically to citizens.

12   Sarah Besky, lecture at RISD Institute for Design and Public Policy, 2016.

13   "Useful" is broadly defined here to mean anything from economic value to delight.

14   See Nesta (2011) for an in-depth analysis of the topic.

15   For instance, the Stanford D School.

16   More from Laura Bunt at NESTA can be found here:
      www.nesta.org.uk/blog/designing-beta-public-service-finding-courage-be-imperfect.

17   The What Works Centre for Wellbeing is a cross-sector approach to improving wellbeing working with national, devolved and local government, voluntary charities and the social enterprise sector and business.

18   For example, systems biology, systems medicine, phenotypes and Bayesian studies (such as clinical trials).

References

Ackoff, R.L. (1981), *Creating the Corporate Future: Plan or be Planned for*. Wiley & Sons, New York.

Argyris, C. and D.A. Schön (1978), *Organizational Learning: A Theory of Action Perspective* (Vol. 173). Addison-Wesley, Reading, MA.

Austin, J.L. (1962), *Sense and Sensibilia* (ed. G.J. Warnock). Oxford, Oxford University Press, Oxford, UK.

Ashby, W.R. (1956), An Introduction to Cybernetics. Chapman and Hall, London.

Berger, W. (2012), "The secret phrase top innovators use", *Harvard Business News*, 17 September 2012, https://hbr.org/2012/09/the-secret-phrase-top-innovato.

Boisot, M. and B. McKelvey (2011), "Connectivity, extremes, and adaptation: A power-law perspective of organizational effectiveness", *Journal of Management Inquiry*, Vol. 20, No. 2, pp. 119-133.

Boyer, B., J. Cook and M. Steinberg (2013), *Legible Practises: Six Stories About the Craft of Stewardship*. SITRA, http://helsinkidesignlab.org/legiblepractises.

Brown, T. (2008), "Design thinking", *Harvard Business Review*, Vol. 86/6, p. 84.

Brown, T. and J. Wyatt (2010), "Design thinking for social innovation", *Stanford Social Innovation Review*, Winter 2010, www.ssireview.org/articles/entry/design_thinking_for_social_innovation.

Buchanan, R. (2001), "Design research and the new learning", *Design issues*, Vol. 17/4, pp. 3-23.

Callon, M., P. Lascoumes and Y. Barthe (2009), *Acting in an Uncertain World*. MIT Press, Cambridge, MA.

Casti, J. (2012), X-Events: Complexity Overload and the Collapse of Everything. William Morrow, New York.

CoLab (2016), *Follow the Rabbit: A Field Guide to Systemic Design*. Government of Alberta, Edmonton, Canada, https://drive.google.com/file/d/0B0KwcwVigAntYm00Tzl4WnZTX0k/view.

Cooper, R., S. Junginger and T. Lockwood (2009), "Design thinking and design management: A research and practice perspective", *Design Management Review*, Vol. 20/2, pp. 46-55.

Demos Helsinki (2015a), "This is why Helsinki is able to implement the basic income experiment", 8 December 2015, Demos Helsinki, www.demoshelsinki.fi/en/2015/12/08/this-is-why-finland-is-able-to-implement-the-basic-income-experiment.

Demos Helsinki (2015b), *Design for Government: Human-centric Governance Through Experiments*, Government's Analysis, Assessment and Research Activities, www.demoshelsinki.fi/wp-content/uploads/2015/09/Design-for-Government-%E2% 80%93-Governance-through-experiments.pdf.

Dorst, K. (2015), *Frame Innovation: Create New Thinking by Design*. MIT Press, Cambridge.

Dorst, K. and L. Royakkers (2006), "The design analogy: A model for moral problem solving", *Design Studies*, Vol. 27/6, pp. 633-656.

Dunne, D. and R. Martin (2006), "Design thinking and how it will change management education: An interview and discussion", *Academy of Management Learning and Education*, Vol. 5/4, pp. 512-523.

Gharajedaghi, J. (2011), Systems Thinking: Managing Chaos and Complexity: A Platform for Designing Business Architecture. Morgan Kaufmann, Burlington, MA.

Helsinki Design Labs (2013), *Hybrid Forums for Urban Controversies: the Ten Commandments.* Helsinki Design Labs, Helsinki, www.helsinkidesignlab.org/blog/hybrid-forums-for-urban-controversies-the-ten-commandments.

Hodgson, A. and G. Leicester (2016), *Second-Order Science and Policy: An Account of the Exploratory Forum*, SITRA/IFF, Helsinki, www.decisionintegrity.co.uk/SOSP%20Report%20Final%20June%202016.pdf.

Ito, J. (2016), "Design and science", *Journal of Design and Science,* http://jods.mitpress.mit.edu/pub/designandscience.

Junginger, S. (2014), "Human-centered design: Integrating systems & services around people by providing a common ground for action", in L. Freund and W. Cellary (eds.), *Advances in the Human Side of Service Engineering*. AHFE Conference, Danvers, MA.

Kelley, D. and G. VanPatter (2005), *Design as Glue: Understanding the Stanford D-school*. NextDesign Leadership Institute, New York.

Lapidos, J. (2009), Why did It take Google so long to take Gmail Out of 'beta'?", *Slate*, 7 July 2009, www.slate.com/articles/news_and_politics/recycled/2009/07/why_did_it_take_google _so_long_to_take_gmail_out_of_beta.html.

Li, M. (2002), "Fostering design culture through cultivating the user-designers' design thinking and systems thinking", *Systemic Practice and Action Research*, Vol. 15/5, pp. 385-410.

Martin, R. (2009), The Design of Business: Why Design Thinking is the Next Competitive Advantage. Harvard Business Press, Boston, MA.

McKelvey, B. and M. Boisot (2009), "Redefining strategic foresight: 'Fast' and 'far' sight via complexity science", in L.A. Costanzo and R.B. MacKay (eds), *Handbook of Research on Strategy and Foresight*. Edward Elgar, Cheltenham, UK, pp. 15-47.

Mulgan, G. (2014), Design in Public and Social Innovation: What Works and What Could Work Better. NESTA, London, www.nesta.org.uk/sites/default/files/design_what_works_what_could_work_better.pdf

Puttick, R., P. Baeck and P. Colligan (2014), *i-teams; The Teams and Funds Making Innovation Happen in Governments Around the World*. NESTA, London, http://theiteams.org/system/files_force/i-teams_June%202014.pdf.

NESTA (2011), *Prototyping Public Services*, NESTA, London, www.nesta.org.uk/sites/default/files/prototyping_public_services.pdf.

Rowe, P.G. (1987), *Design Thinking MIT Press*. Cambridge, MA.

Simpson, I. (2011), "Ethnography: Caught between myths", *Research Live*, 25 February 2011, www.research-live.com/article/opinion/ethnography-caught-between-myths/id/4004640.

Smith, H. (2015), "People are still living in FEMA's toxic Katrina trailers — and they likely have no idea", *Grist,* 27 August 2015, http://grist.org/politics/people-are-still-living-in-femas-toxic-katrina-trailers-and-they-likely-have-no-idea.

Tõnurist, P., R. Kattel and V. Lember (2015), "Discovering innovation labs in the public sector", *The Other Canon and Tallinn University Working Papers in Technology Governance and Economic Dynamics*, Vol. 61, June, https://pdfs.semanticscholar.org/adc5/021cb863d386401f5b8221185ad565beb89b.pdf.

Wastell, D. (2010), "Managing as designing: 'opportunity knocks' for the IS field?", *European Journal of Information Systems*, Vol. 19/4, pp. 422-431.

Further reading

Donahue, A. and R. Tuohy (2006), "Lessons we don't learn: A study of the lessons of disasters, why we repeat them, and how we can learn them", *Homeland Security Affairs*, Vol. 2/2.

Vickers, G. (1970), *Freedom in a Rocking Boat*. Penguin Books, London.

Von Foerster, H. (2003), "Ethics and second-order cybernetics", in *Understanding Understanding*. Springer, New York, pp. 287-304.

Chapter 3.

System approaches in practice: Case studies

This chapter provides an in-depth examination of four systemic change case studies from diverging contexts. It analyses how systems approaches have been applied in practice to: prevent domestic violence (Iceland), protect children (the Netherlands), regulate the sharing economy (Canada) and design a policy framework for conducting experiments in government (Finland). The case studies provide an overview of the context of the change process, steps to initiate and carry out systems change, and its impacts. The chapter highlights the complexity in terms of problems examined and government levels involved, and the difficulties of working across silos. The cases show that systems approaches can be very beneficial in redefining government outcomes and structuring change, but that transformation also requires various resources, such as flexible finances, time, political coverage, systems thinking capabilities, and independent brokers. The empirical examination also reveals the ongoing need of systems thinking and iterative processes as implementing systems change invariably unearths unforeseen effects, system barriers highlighting the need for meaningful measurement of outcome-oriented change.

The following cases studies of systems change were developed in accordance with the protocol described in Annex 3. The selection process examined fifteen different initiatives from across the world and selected four exploratory case studies for in-depth analysis. Case studies characterised by a high form of variety – both in terms of the methodological tools employed and the government levels involved – were preferred. In some of the cases, systems and design approaches were not explicitly employed (such as Iceland), however the processes used and outcomes were systemic in nature. In other cases (such as Canada), systems thinking and design methods were formally adopted.

A systems approach to tackling domestic violence: The United Against Domestic Violence programme (Iceland)

Summary

The Icelandic government is implementing a programme to address violence against women. The programme introduces a new integrated support system for victims based on the concept that domestic violence is a social (and not private) harm that affects everyone. The programme was prompted by an early pilot in the southern region of Suðurnes. Following research findings on domestic violence, and supported by new legislation, the programme sets out a radical systems change that centres support around the victim and concentrates on stabilising the family, rather than focusing on providers and authorities (lawyers, police, social services, etc.). Today, the police, social and child protective services (and increasingly schools and healthcare providers) are working in a coordinated fashion to detect and respond effectively to domestic violence across Iceland.

Context

The region of Suðurnes is located on the south-western edge of Iceland and is home to the nation's second-largest settlement (numbering approx. 22 000 in 2015) and the Keflavík International Airport. Until 2006, it hosted the Keflavík US Naval Air Station established during the Second World War to protect the Atlantic interests of allied forces. The Air Station was the region's largest employer providing jobs for approximately 900 Icelanders who supplied material and support services to the base and the Iceland Defence Force stationed there. The closure of the base occurred with little warning and sent shockwaves throughout the community. It contributed to the highest unemployment rate in Iceland, a problem that was further exacerbated by the financial crisis of 2008.

The station closure and financial crisis compounded social difficulties in Suðurnes, which has nearly twice the national rate of immigrants and many young parents. Unemployment rates and the number of families receiving financial benefits were high. In addition, research conducted by the Ministry of Welfare in response to a 2006 government action plan showed that Suðurnes had the highest level of domestic violence in the country, while the rate was consistently lower across the rest of Iceland.

Gender inequality has long been highlighted as the most significant driver of violence against women (Kyvsgaard and Snare, 2007), while lifestyle factors such as income, work and so on play a lesser role. If this theory is true, then Iceland should enjoy the lowest rate of domestic violence in Europe. In 2010, the World Economic Forum published a study that ranked Iceland first for gender equality worldwide, in spite of the fact that the government's own 2008 research found domestic violence in the country to be on a par with other similarly developed nations. Thus, from a classical public health perspective, Suðurnes was an exception: prevalence of violence should have been more or less consistent with the country as a whole. While current research suggests that lifestyle factors play a more significant role, the government's research drew significant national attention to the region along with pressure for improvement.

In order to shift public discourse, the Icelandic government's 2006 action plan to address domestic violence introduced a moral imperative of zero tolerance. However, long-term direct and indirect costs to society resulting from domestic violence also needed to be addressed. A study by the Council of Europe (2014) cited alarming realities in the domain of domestic violence, as well as significant costs arising from lack of violence prevention. Overall, the study found that while awareness, policy and legislation had improved efforts to curb violence, there remained significant gaps between incidence levels and conviction rates. This enforcement gap also surfaced in Iceland. A Suðurnes Police analysis showed that out of 18 cases of domestic violence brought to the police in 2011, 17 investigations were discontinued (mostly due to retracted statements by the victims) and the remaining case was dropped by prosecutors after being determined unlikely to succeed in court. These case numbers are low, but in the minds of police and prosecutors they reflected a worrying trend. Since 2003, 40% of homicide cases in Iceland were thought to be the result of violence in intimate relationships. The Suðurnes data suggested that the current system was unlikely to produce results in terms of limiting the escalation of violence (e.g. preventing homicides) stemming from domestic violence detection or prosecution, simply because perpetrators were not being brought to justice. According to current and former Suðurnes authorities, the risk felt more imminent, particularly in a small country, as any of the dropped investigations could escalate into a homicide. The gap between prevalence (the pervasiveness of offences) and prosecution indicted the current system. Detection, interdiction, support, treatment and criminal justice were present as services, but were not aligned toward common means and ends.

Domestic violence also places a significant economic burden on society. According to the Council of Europe report, while it is difficult to measure the total "costs" of violence against women, cost categories include:

> *Increased burdens on law enforcement structures, costs linked to the judiciary (civil, criminal and administrative), legal costs incurred by an individual party, health care costs, housing and shelters, lost wages and/or decrease in taxes paid to the state due to reduced employment and productivity, social services for women and their children, income support and other support services (2014: 1).*

Extensive as this list is, it does not include long-term costs, especially to children, who when exposed to violence in the home tend to repeat the behaviour later in life creating a vicious cycle. As one senior official pointed out, the toxic stress experienced by children exposed to violence in the home can mirror similar negative effects of children raised in war zones.

Costs for an event (or series of events) such as domestic violence are notoriously difficult to calculate. Some national studies have nevertheless been conducted and aggregated by the Council of Europe. The results show that the effects of violence are complex and vary widely based on how the research was structured and the kinds of services available to victims. One study from Finland estimated the cost to be EUR 101 million in 1998, or about EUR 20 per capita. An EU 25 study estimated domestic violence costs to be EUR 16 billion in 2006, or EUR 35 per capita among the 25 member states. In the United States, estimates show that domestic violence costs USD 8.3 billion annually in direct costs and lost productivity (CAEPV, n.d.). In Iceland, understanding costs proved an important element in raising awareness and motivating action. Moreover, in a small country, "the lines of communication are very short"[1] and the toll of violence can be harder to ignore.

Prior to recognition of this growing problem, the authorities in Suðurnes managed domestic violence incidents through various administrative silos. In emergent situations, the police would respond to a call from a victim or relative to ensure public safety and stop any ongoing violence, but would not generally treat the home as a crime scene or conduct an investigation (this could explain in part why few cases ended in conviction much less a formal charge). Social services were sometimes involved in an active interdiction, but typically followed up with support services once the acute phase had already passed. Child protective services would be called if a child was present and he or she was obviously impacted by the event. However, the three service arms were not coordinated through a response or action protocol. Responsibility to determine what was necessary and when to take action was largely left to the police. In most cases, victims would not make additional requests beyond the initial intervention.

In the context of laws prior to 2011, this arrangement was natural. While the National Commissioner had implemented new procedures for domestic violence in 2005, police authorities in local practise did not work in accordance with these procedures until the programme began. The key factor from the authorities' perspective in domestic violence cases, other than public safety, was the location. For instance, a case of assault between two people in an intimate relationship would be treated differently (classified as assault, not domestic violence) if it occurred in a restaurant versus the home. Thus, it was not clear how to define cases as domestic violence or disputes (this changed during the course of the project). Domestic violence was also not recognised as an offence under the Icelandic penal code, but as a component of several other kinds of violations (e.g. assault, sex crimes, etc.), if an intimate relationship existed between the victim and the accused. This registration structure limited the police's ability to track prevalence and conviction rates and created inconsistencies in how cases were handled. Withdrawal of claims was common and even those that were pursued often lacked complete information, all of which contributed to a particularly damaging situation where repeat offenders were unlikely to be convicted. At a more abstract level, it reinforced the compartmentalisation of domestic violence as a private matter that did not rise to the level of other forms of violence or necessitate the development of a coordinated, preventative response.

However, following the government's 2006 domestic violence action plan, a new law (No. 85/2011) was approved in 2011 with the aim of providing authorities with more tools to protect victims. The law was based on an Austrian precedent that permitted authorities to remove offenders from the home and place a specific restraining order on them when domestic violence was suspected. Previously, the onus to request a restraining order or remove a violent individual from the home fell on the victim, who would rarely demand either intervention. Furthermore, when a restraining order was requested, the administrative process could take up to a week and was determined at the discretion of the regional chief of police and finally by a judge. These factors could bias the outcome of an intervention towards the concerns of law enforcement and the judicial system, rather than addressing the complex, emergent needs of a victim or mitigate broader social harms.

It is important in the context of this case study to recognise that while Iceland's pre-2011 system of detecting and responding to domestic violence provided limited support to victims, it seemed natural, normal and, to many, sufficient at the time. It was not designed in this manner because of a lack of sympathy or concern for victims. In fact, it was never designed. The system evolved over time in response to social norms, advocacy (or lack thereof), budgeting decisions and other dynamics into a structure where domestic violence was not considered sufficiently serious and the victim was solely responsible for pushing the matter forward.

Initiating a process of systems change

In the wake of the 2011 law, which provided authorities with more provisions to protect victims, the Suðurnes police initiated a special investigation to assess the response to the high incidence of domestic violence in Iceland. The findings were disconcerting:

- Few domestic violence cases successfully passed through the justice system due to incomplete investigations, and only a small number of perpetrators were convicted.

- The police rarely used restraining orders or expelled perpetrators from homes.

- There were few available forms of support for victims or perpetrators.

- Cooperation among police, social services and child protective services was minimal.[2]

For the police, the facts suggested that they were "not doing their job properly" and that dramatic, systemic change was needed. Following such a determination, the next steps can often seem unclear or impossible. But in a small district like Suðurnes, teamwork is a normal practice, which made collaboration on an issue at a systemic, cross-silo level with key stakeholders relatively straightforward. The police began by arranging a meeting with representatives from the health and social services, as well as the church, to discuss what could be done. After a few additional meetings, a decision was taken to launch a one-year pilot project called *Keeping a Window Open* to bring the police and social services into closer cooperation. The title of the project referred to the window of opportunity open in the immediate aftermath of domestic violence, when an intervention can achieve its greatest impact. Rather than abiding by an administrative timeline, the police and social services would work to achieve as much as possible while the window was open. This approach represented a significant departure from the common, transactional practice of simply removing a perpetrator from the scene.

The rationale underpinning the pilot project was that victims' needs could be better met through a coordinated, rapid intervention that would effectively provide "wraparound" services. This intervention would be designed to yield stronger evidence to improve the likelihood of a future conviction. Ultimately, it would shift the design and delivery of the domestic violence "system" from an institutional architecture to a human-centred architecture. While this systems language was not used by the Suðurnes Police and their partners at the time, systems concepts were nevertheless embedded in their project.

A systems approach was achieved by developing a specific set of aims that responded to the failures identified in the government's research and the police's special investigation married to a set of organising principles such as zero tolerance, social harm, the right to freedom from violence, gender equality and so on. The institutional boundaries that would normally govern the structure of public policy or even experimental pilot projects were minimised, not as an explicit attempt at de-siloisation, but more as a matter of local practice among a small network of actors.

However, the organising theme of the Suðurnes pilot was clearly systemic: "the whole system needed to take domestic violence much more seriously" from the first indication of a problem. Other aims such as preventing repeat offenders and increased prosecution rates would also accrue systemic benefits. The tools employed in the pilot included:

- a thorough crime scene investigation

- recorded testimony on scene

- a medical examination by a doctor

- social services referral

- use of legal provisions such as restraining orders and home expulsions

- provision of support to victims

- a follow-up visit to the home within one week

- a panic button to alert police and risk assessment.

In practice, this meant that rather than one to two officers arriving on scene, a consortium of seven to eight people would intervene including four uniformed officers, a detective, social services, child protective services and so on. Lawyers and additional service providers would be on call 24 hours a day. Once an incidence of domestic violence was detected, the police would contact social services immediately to begin the process.

At its core, the pilot would require deep cooperation between police and social services; however, current regulations imposed some limitations. A social worker is automatically called to the scene in every case where children are listed in the home or present at home. But in cases where children are not involved, police are required to receive at least verbal consent from the victims to call a social worker. In most cases (about 90%), the victims are in such need of assistance by the time they call the police, that they are relieved to have a social worker on scene and provide consent immediately. Experience has shown that cooperation with the victim improves when social workers are involved from the beginning and that victims were more likely to go to a doctor for a medical examination under the escort of a social worker. Under these conditions, the victim would receive better support and critical evidence was more likely to be obtained by the authorities in order to make a successful prosecution.

After much planning, the *Keeping a Window Open* pilot was launched on 1 February 2013. At that time, Sigríður Björk Guðjónsdóttir was the Chief of Police, Skúli Jónsson was the Superintendent and Alda Hrönn Jóhannsdóttir was Head of the Legal Department of Suðurnes Police (lawyer) and Deputy Chief of Police. Jóhannsdóttir (legal department) and Jónsson (uniformed police) together with Superintendent Jóhannes Jensson (investigative police) formed the "Three Amigos", a group charged with pushing the process forward. This steering function included new protocol training, introducing the *social harm* concept into the police mind-set, public awareness and process refinement.

The mental models that arise from training, routine and group norms are some of the most stable (and therefore stubborn) elements of complex social systems. The Suðurnes police were no exception, largely because of habit. However, as one observer shared:

Superintendent Jónsson was really great: a male voice following up with the work [of the pilot]. If there was resistance from policemen then he spoke to everyone one-on-one asking, "Why are you complaining? We are changing, why are you not changing?"

As this quote suggests, gender – a critical component of authority (witness the topic of this case study) – played a role in shifting the group norms of the predominantly male police department. Chief Guðjónsdóttir had worked in the department since 2007 and was the first female Deputy National Commissioner in Iceland – a challenging position in the best of circumstances.[3] The Three Amigos leadership structure combined with the Deputy Chief's hands-on approach played an important strategic role in shifting norms within the department. But effective backing among senior leadership and the people was critical:

Sigríður, as the Chief of Police in the District, had a big role in the project. She pushed us forward and as you know if you do not have support from your boss, you are not likely to succeed.

An important aspect of shifting from a siloed to a human-centric service delivery model was developing means by which the new consortium would increase the area of contact between support services and victims. Victims and their circumstances and contexts are highly varied. This presents a challenge to public sector institutions, which have long understood their citizens in single dimensions defined by administrative authority. At a pragmatic level in Suðurnes, this required extending engagement with victims beyond the acute crisis in order to better understand the situation and calibrate needs to the available services.

Within one week of a domestic violence incident, a Suðurnes police detective and social worker would perform a follow-up visit with the aim of understanding how the situation had progressed and if the violence had continued. Following the visit, a report would be prepared that would help the police assess if there was ongoing violence. Prohibited entry or a non-answer was often a good indicator of an ongoing problem. During this first week, social workers would also visit the perpetrator to offer assistance, such as referral to state-subsidised counselling. Outcomes from these visits would be carefully recorded to develop data that would help the consortium better understand the nature of domestic violence and how services provided relief, supply evidence for future trials and assess how the pilot itself was performing. The Suðurnes Police also developed a set of risk factors to help them anticipate if a case might represent an ongoing problem. These factors included analysis of the probability for escalating violence, repeated offenses, and a need for a restraining order or expulsion from the home.

The pilot consortium worked to change mind-sets about domestic violence internally, but also recognised the need to raise awareness among the public in the region. Following the launch of the pilot, they published a brochure in three languages entitled *Is Domestic Violence a Part of Your Life?* Recognising the police's limited intelligence regarding where domestic violence was occurring, they distributed copies to all households in the Suðurnes region with the support of the Ministry of Welfare and the Welfare Department in Suðurnes, of which Superintentent Jónsson was a member on behalf of the Suðurnes Police. Social workers also began working with teachers and staff in schools to recognise some of the indicators of domestic violence and to explain what they can do if children share pertinent information. In parallel, the consortium launched a public information campaign in the press and gave lectures to socialise and strengthen the concept of domestic violence as a form of social harm.

The law was another critical medium through which transformative change was pursued. For Suðurnes Police General Counsel, Alda Hrönn, the guiding principle was that the law must be suitable for the needs of the victim, not tailored to the *needs* of the system. In her view, the law was not immutable, but the human rights of domestic violence victims were. This provided an orientation for existing statutes and decisions made by the courts, which could help her assess how well existing laws were aligned with the concept of social harm. Having represented victims of domestic violence, she found very little grey area in terms of her clients' wellbeing. For Alda, the purpose of the law was crystal clear: to protect women and children, both of whom are predominantly the victims of violence.

By testing the limits of the law and working to reorganise it around the interests of victims, the work of the Suðurnes pilot could be made more durable and transferable to other regions. Alda and her colleagues understood that the creation of legal precedents resulted in progress in legal and broader systems.

A final, critical layer of initiating the new process was to build a mechanism by which the consortium could learn by doing. Every two weeks, the uniformed and investigative police, social services and health services would meet to share information, refine practices, and strengthen the social and working relationship of the consortium. In practice, this meant reviewing the current case load, considering available remedies when a victim is believed to still be in danger, discussing shortcomings in cooperative practices, and determining how to respond as a group to new procedures and directives from the National Commissioner of the Police. As with Morbidity and Mortality conferences (M&Ms) in academic hospitals, the consortium's bi-weekly meetings brought together separate administrative silos (medical specialities in the case of hospitals and public service departments in Suðurnes) as peers with a shared objective of improving practices and developing greater understanding and alignment. This was particularly important in helping the consortium detect and work to resolve systems issues such as gaps in services or legacy policies that are no longer relevant.

Meetings such as M&Ms consume time and resources and can seem unnecessary, especially to functional areas whose tasks and administrative authority are well defined. Furthermore, it can be tempting to dispense with these meetings once a development phase is largely over. However, when working in complex emergent systems, such meetings are critical to maintaining the relevance, flexibility and efficacy of an intervention such as the Suðurnes pilot. From a planning perspective, time and space must be allocated to perform the work of systems change, such as through social learning processes like M&Ms. As one member of the consortium shared, "To do this kind of change, you need to have the people who have the time to do the work right. No one can do it alone".

Impacts and systems effects

The impact of the *Keeping a Window Open* pilot is visible in the case statistics assembled by the Suðurnes Police. Between 2010 and September 2015 (the date of last available statistics), more cases resulted in police interventions and more investigations are being referred to the courts (Figure 3.1).

Figure 3.1. Domestic violence cases, Suðurnes, 2010-2015

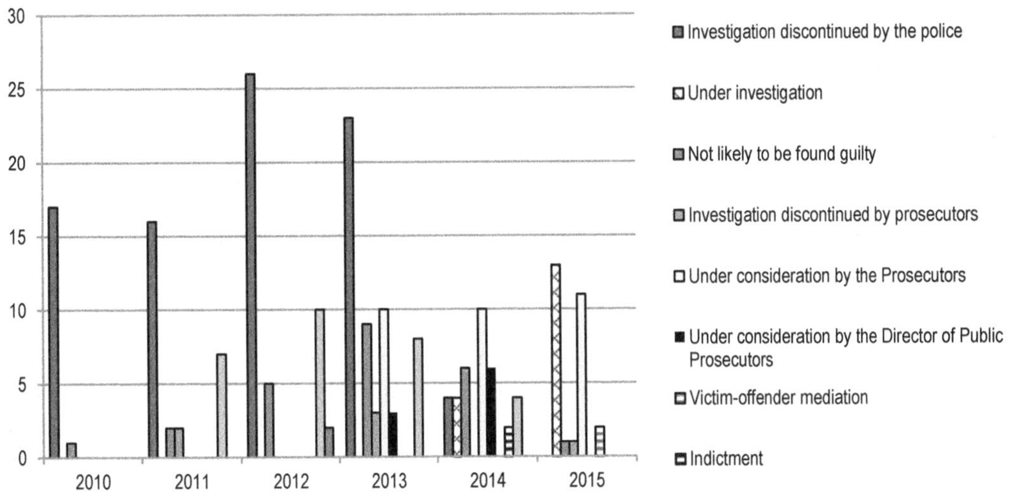

Source: Jónsson and Einarsdóttir (2016).

A higher caseload suggests that public awareness about domestic violence is increasing, as economic and other social factors remained relatively stable in the region. Better registration of cases also explains, in part, the increase in cases seen in 2012. More cases making it to the courts and resulting in prosecution suggests that better evidence is being generated and possibly that the attitude of the legal system is changing vis-à-vis domestic violence. Further analysis will be needed to determine correlation/causation, but what is clear is that the system has become more responsive to the issue of domestic violence. Remarkably, this impact was achieved with no additional budget for the pilot, as the existing budget was reprioritised to cover additional activities and costs.

Following the successful one-year pilot in Suðurnes, the National Commissioner of Police issued new national procedures in December 2014 based on *Keeping a Window Open*. Since that time, all police districts across Iceland have adopted a similar approach with local variations based on municipal infrastructure, size of the population and so on. Meanwhile, in Suðurnes, practices, knowledge and partnerships continue to be refined. Once ten years of data has been accumulated, the authorities hope to have a clear picture of what worked in the project and what remains to be done. In the meantime, they are working to strengthen information sharing by working closely with health services and schools. Privacy protection remains a key systemic barrier to greater fluidity and transmission of data between hospitals, schools and the original partners of the consortium.

Suðurnes Police Chief Guðjónsdóttir has since been appointed Chief of the Reykjavik Metropolitan Police, the largest municipality in Iceland, and continues her work on domestic violence there with Alda Hrönn as Chief Attorney for the police. The City of Reykjavik has also established a steering committee for domestic violence housed in the city's Office of Human Rights. They are tasked broadly with carrying forward the work of transforming what was once a private issue into a public issue with the support of political leadership. The Office of Human Rights provides a neutral territory to help the committee navigate complex administrative silos in the city. Challenges continue to arise in part due to a dynamic context (i.e. changing demographics) and also because of greater clarity regarding the complexity of domestic violence and how institutions respond, neither of which could have been easily foreseen.

For instance, prior to the project, the Reykjavik police called child protective services in only a few cases. Now, they are summoned in nearly every case due to the presence of children at the scene. The social services are also called to the scene if children are registered in the home, even if they are not present at the time. The child protective services are always notified in such cases, although they do not come to the scene when children are not at home, and intervene thereafter if needed. This has led to a massive caseload increase for the authorities, with the associated risk of burnout and declining job satisfaction. As a result, the city and state will likely need to deploy more resources.

In 2017, a new approach entitled Birch House was launched in Reykjavik to provide a "one-stop shop" for victims of domestic violence. Birch House brings together all the city's social services and emergency housing resources under one roof, in order to provide true wraparound support for victims and their families. This new project signals the replacement of administrative silos (from the perspective of the "user") with a single service platform. It also represents a significant advancement on the concepts initiated by the Suðurnes consortium. While this approach may not be viable in other, less populated areas, Birch House points to an entirely different approach to domestic violence and speaks to the promise of moving systems toward human centricity. As one observer noted, "We have seen a big difference in culture and priorities within the system."

In 2016, the Institute for Gender, Equality and Difference at the University of Iceland conducted a study of the project to better determine its effect on survivors, police, social services, child protective services and perpetrators. This kind of project is inherently difficult to evaluate because it involves a complex intervention into a complex community, and entails multiple sources of both qualitative and quantitative data. Nevertheless, the evaluators set out to better understand whether the system was better serving victims and perpetrators, whether authorities were collaborating more effectively, whether children were better equipped to live with violence, and whether public discussion had changed with respect to domestic violence. Overall, victims were satisfied with the performance of police and social workers. Most police officers were also satisfied with the programme and thought it was well designed to meet the needs of victims. Social services had a very positive view of the project with 93.5% of respondents believing it was good for survivors.

Critically, social services and police both felt that collaboration was working and improving with each case (see Figure 3.2). However, there are also challenges. Police and social services feel that their workload has increased significantly, which risks burnout, and indicates a need to re-evaluate resourcing. In addition, the crucial follow-up visit needs to be redesigned to be more effective.

Figure 3.2. Together Against Domestic Violence evaluation

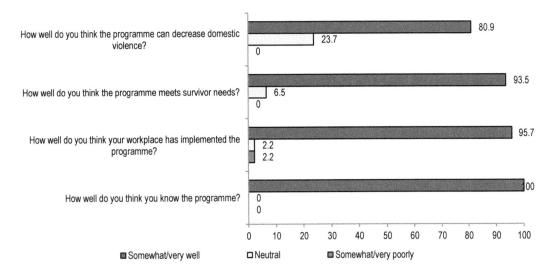

Source: Sigurvinsdóttir (2016).

Work continues in Iceland to combat domestic violence at a systemic level. In 2014, the total number of domestic disturbances cases was 799 (both disputes and domestic violence), while the number of reported domestic violence cases was 294. In 2015, the total number of domestic disturbances cases rose to 1 213, the number of disputes cases was 606 cases, and the number of domestic violence cases was 607. These statistics represent an enormous increase in reporting of domestic violence cases. The effect of systemic changes on addressing domestic violence continues to be monitored, with a view to providing a better assessment of the contribution of systems change to preventing domestic violence and providing effective support to victims.

Using system approaches in policy design: introducing experimental culture as a high-level political goal (Finland)

Summary

In 2015, Finland started to develop a new framework for experimental policy design. Together with Demos Helsinki, a Nordic think tank, the Prime Minister's Office (PMO) of Finland employed a combined systems and design thinking approach in order to develop a new policy framework to carry out experiments in government. In parallel, key figures of the ruling Centre Party were involved with developing and spreading the idea of "experimental culture" in the Parliament of Finland. As a result, experimentation was incorporated into the strategic government programme ("Finland, a land of Solutions") in May 2015 and an experimental policy design programme was set up. The new approach to policy design allowed both broader "strategic experiments" (formalised policy trials) – for example, the ongoing basic income experiment – and a grassroots experiment designed to build up an "experimental culture" in the public sector in Finland. In addition to the original six strategic experiments introduced by the government, hundreds of experiments and policy pilots are emerging across the country both at the central government and municipal level. In 2017, the Finnish government is launching a digital platform called *Kokeilun Paikka*[4] (Place to Experiment) to support the government's key goal: finding innovative ways to develop public services.

Context

Finland has engaged in the debate on systems change in government as part of its Governments for the Future (2012-2014) project. The project was launched by the Ministry of Finance and the Prime Minister's Office in partnership with SITRA (the fund for innovation operating directly under the Finnish Parliament) to discover new ways to execute significant state administration reforms.

In 2012, the Committee of the Future in the Parliament held hearings regarding new methods of steering and strategy for the country. One participant noted that, "there was a general feeling in the parliament that they were far removed from what was going on – there were a lot of discussions, but very little action". One topic presented at the committee, "experimental culture" – based on sustainability and environmental experiments – provoked a lot of interest across party lines. In response, the committee commissioned a special report, *Kokeilun paikka! Suomi matkalla kohti kokeiluyhteiskuntaa* ("Time to Experiment! Finland on its way to the Experimental Society") (Berg, 2013), which argued for rapid iteration, grassroots experiments and a strategic outlook focused on experimentation in government. The report also suggested the creation of an office or ombudsman for experimentation and public sector innovation. Juha Sipilä, who in 2015 became Prime Minister of Finland, was then a parliamentarian and heavily involved in the work as a member of the committee. This process created initial political buy-in for experimentation in government, and it was especially fortuitous that the future Prime Minister was directly involved in the work. As one commentator noted, "I don't know if the approach would have been promoted at the PMO's level at such a pace if they [hadn't] made it their theme to promote". As the idea took root, several other reports on experimentation in public policy were published in Finland (e.g. Berg et al., 2014).

In parallel, the government initiated the OHRA Project (2014) – a steering framework – to prepare recommendations for the next parliamentary term after the elections in the first quarter of 2015, in order to improve the impact and effectiveness of government actions. The OHRA activities identified the horizontal nature of many new policy problems, the lack of an evidence base in policy making, and the gap in the feedback loop within the policy-making system from policy implementation to policy design. Finland was seen as a "legalistic society" where regulation was used as the main vehicle of change. As one observer noted: "Lawyers and social scientists do not come together in our policy-making system, the collaboration is not deep enough. Thus, there are little alternatives to legislation." More flexible forms of problem solving were therefore deemed necessary. The OHRA project also recommended that the government programme become more strategic. The final report proposed that a major part of the research funding supporting government decision making (the so-called TEAS function)[5] should be allocated to the needs of the Government Action Plan (ibid.). The resources for the Experimental Finland team and its activities were allotted from the government's research and assessment team's budget, both of which form part of the Prime Minister's Office's share of the state budget. By the end of the process there was a high level of consensus regarding how to develop the policy-making process in Finland.

This was the context in which the PMO began to look for new tools to improve the government's steering framework. The Office was especially interested in the upcoming fields of behavioural insights, experimentation and evidence-based policy making. Thus, the PMO drafted a tender focusing on ways to implement these fields. Two different theoretical sources were merged for the experimental policy design programme: behavioural economics-based thinking (e.g. randomised control trials (RCTs) and the Behavioural Insights Team (BIT) experience from the UK); and the rapid process of experimentation/iteration found in lean start-up thinking, which draws on business experience. As a result, the programme had two different ideas built into it: top-down thinking (RCTs, etc.) and bottom-up thinking (iterative, grassroots-level development work). This approach resulted later in the division of experiments, with large policy trials (formalised RCTs) separated from smaller, bottom-up and intuitive ways of conducting experiments. These different levels of experiments are described here separately to create an understanding of the many levels of experiments and their respective value within the experimental "ecosystem".

Demos Helsinki – a Nordic think tank[6] – focused its proposal on strategic change, won the tender and started work on the framework in early 2015. They proposed a more practical approach, shying away from solely theoretical approaches. Their methodology combined the "traditional literature review" with a co-creation process, the ultimate purpose of which was to produce useful insights that could feed into the government's agenda.

Initiating a process of systems change

Demos Helsinki started their work with a brief of complex topics from the PMO: behavioural insights, evidence-based policy making and experimentation. The government research plan for 2014 identified a key study objective of outlining new policy instruments and support for a culture of experimentation. The PMO wanted to know which experiences had been gained by countries applying a behavioural and experimental approach to policy guidance and what lessons could be learned with a view to developing policy instruments for the government.[7] No single framework existed that took into account all the aforementioned points. Furthermore, the exact nature of the government's demands was unclear. Nevertheless, Demos Helsinki saw a possibility under the initial auspice of behavioural insights to create an opening for feedback mechanisms that would allow for more flexible decision making – an overall new steering framework: "It was not about how good of a report we could write, but the aim was to change the culture/habits of public administration, introduce new methods, decentralize and emancipate citizens." Thus, they aimed to create a framework to test new approaches to policy design and concentrate on the "iterative nature of policy making".

As Demos Helsinki's work did not centre particularly on behavioural insights, they considered all methods, tools and resources (co-creation, etc.) that could steer behaviour and create a "new way of policy making" for a more resilient society. The idea was to create a "Nordic model", which would give power to the citizens. After further work, a "Finnish model" emerged.

Demos Helsinki struggled with the agenda as it was initially defined and, as a result, the project had to be reframed. The initial brief emphasised human-centeredness and behavioural insights, but the goal and research questions were quite broad and allowed for an open approach. Behavioural insights were seen as too complex and general, and did not allow Demos Helsinki to focus. Hence, a strategic choice was made to centre on experimentation. However, the team tried to retain a broader view and "not to love the method too much". Furthermore, experiments (or pilots) were seen as "more understandable" to the general public (denoting broader citizen engagement), which was especially important at the time because Finland was approaching general elections. Thus, while the project started with a strong emphasis on behavioural insights and evidence-based policy design, it culminated with a framework based on experimental policy design.

To arrive at a framework that the public sector could apply, Demos Helsinki adopted a multi-method approach. They carried out an initial review of relevant practices, then interviewed experts from the public, private and third sector; next, they created a community around experimentation, then moved to obtain international validation for the report. Demos Helsinki applied a loose systems design approach to analysing the problem and pulled together different sources to design the experimentation process.

The team first carried out a review of relevant literature in the field including existing benchmark OECD, NESTA and SITRA documents.[8] "We didn't want to come up with something new – just take the findings into the Finnish context." After analysing the working methods of top innovation organisations in the public sector (e.g. Mindlab, BIT, Kennisland, What Works Centre for Aging Better, Policy Lab UK, etc.), the team arrived at the conclusion that the feedback loop in most of these cases was fragmented. Final feedback from the implementation phase did not reach the policy design phase: there was a gap in the process. As one observer noted, "There is no self-evident link in social and health services between implementation and policy design". As a result, feedback from policy implementation did not filter into the process for designing new interventions (see from HOW to WHY in Figure 3.3). Experimentation was seen as a way to build the link between citizens, end-users, stakeholders and policy designers.

Figure 3.3. Policy-making cycle

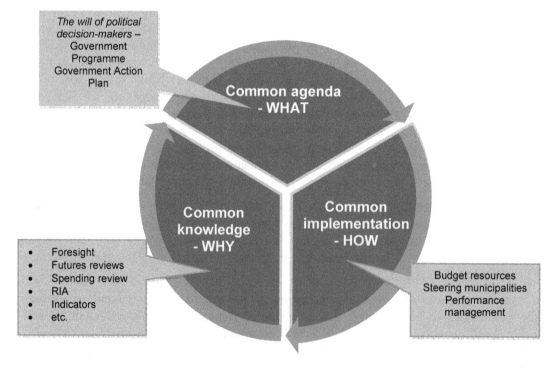

Source: Updated from OHRA Project Group (2014).

Demos Helsinki proceeded to put the different methodologies together and develop a "human-centred model of experimentation". The aim was to make steering mechanisms more effective by using behaviour-based knowledge and develop those mechanisms in collaboration with citizens (see the process outlined in Figure 3.4). The approach concentrated on different iterative phases: selection of a problem, open call for experts and best practices, expert review (taking stock of the existing knowledge base), defining the experiment, qualitative research, validating the experiment and evaluating the experiment. The model in itself is intuitive in nature and does not introduce novelty to the process of experimentation; but the report itself put the process in the Finnish context reflecting the role of local actors and the policy environment. Furthermore, the model assumed the strong presence of an "experiment facilitator".

Figure 3.4. The experimental policy design model

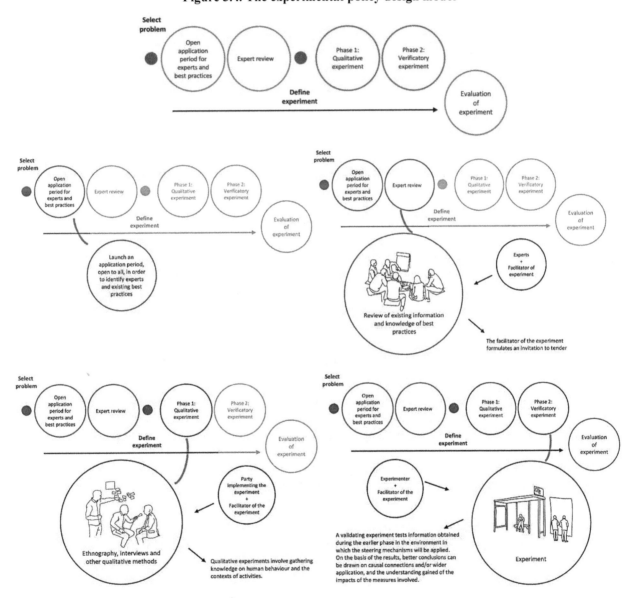

Source: Annala (2016).

In the early version of the report, Demos Helsinki used a traditional Double Diamond model to describe the process of experimentation in government; however, this proved difficult for civil servants to understand. The model was therefore simplified to show different parts of the process and a table simulating the process was created (see Figure 3.5). Traditional forms of representation proved to be most effective with civil servants.

Figure 3.5. Translating the approach to a public sector context: From the Double Diamond to a table-based simulation

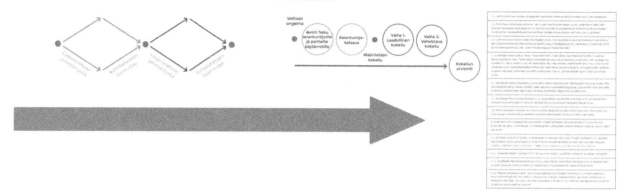

Source: Authors based on Demos Helsinki (2015).

The first draft of the framework was "floated" with political parties in Parliament, three government parties, permanent secretaries, civil servants in workshops and the wider community (NGOs), and international experts. Interviews were carried out with the former and a field trip to London was organised in March 2015. There, the work was presented to international experts and the model was validated (with the participation of BIT, the Design Council, the Cabinet Office, Design Lab, What Works and NESTA). This meeting resulted in the creation of a network inside and outside Finland – later called "the godparents of experimentation" (Kokeilukummit) – who validated the concept. A similar godparent/mentor approach was introduced into the 2015 project to investigate the need and modalities for a specific fund or method for funding small-scale, bottom-up experiments. Such broad validation of the concept helped to create wide-scale acceptance of the approach. As one of the people involved in the process noted, "There was a fair amount of discussion and educating politicians."

Debate was cut short, however, by an opportunity to align the framework with the new government programme. Although the report came out in July 2015,[9] the results had to be presented in mid-March to permanent secretaries, in order to generate discussions on the new programme. As such, the PMO's strategy unit had to develop materials for the new government programme in parallel with Demos Helsinki's work on the report. Both SITRA and Demos Helsinki were involved in the process and encouraged the government to set new objectives. Timing was key.

> *Timing is everything – election and the negotiations – otherwise, with the prior OHRA discussions, it could have actually been a very internal process and the experimentation could have ended with a more lab-type solution.*

In order to leave room for debate, the draft report avoided stipulating strong or overly specific measures for implementing the experimental policy design programme. It outlined the steps of the programme itself, delineated the role of experimentation facilitators (but did not indicate the need for a special unit for experimentation) and proposed a two-year implementation period. With broader consensus, backing from the new prime minister and the work of the PMO, the new government programme placed special attention on changing working methods. This became one of six main blocks of activities in the government programme that merged together deregulation, digitalisation and experimentation. For the first time, a truly strategic government programme existed that included "a story for the government, a vision for the next ten years and a plan of action for the four-year term."

The need to advance the schedule unfortunately reduced the time available for some of the planned groundwork for the programme. Demos Helsinki wanted to liaise with Aalto University's Design for Government course, which was running concurrently, but the timelines did not match. The course takes students from different fields – engineers, designers, etc. – in order to analyse different services and systems within the public sector (e.g. students visualised public R&D transactions, outlined the architecture of agricultural subsidies and debated nudging for healthier eating in schools). However, Demos Helsinki's report still cited the course as an example of insourcing ideas.

While the work of Demos Helsinki was fast-tracked, they also conducted follow-up projects and produced reports connected to the programme (regarding funding of experiments, an ethical code of conduct, etc.) (Demos Helsinki, 2016). Their continuing involvement in the process enabled them to brief the PMO, leading to stronger recommendations being debated regarding implementation of the programme after the report was de facto completed. Pushing the agenda forward created a new legal basis for experimentation – evaluated on a case-by-case basis – in the public sector; meanwhile, the Prime Minister's Office set up an internal Experimental Finland Team, which started working in 2016 (see Experimental Finland, 2016).

Experimental culture within a governmental programme creates a strong and effective "license to experiment" at all levels of government. The creation of Experimental Finland Team within the Prime Minister's Office was designed to support the implementation of strategic experiments and a policy of "experimental culture" in accordance with the government programme. The programme also set up a parliamentary advisory group to legitimise action at the highest level. As a result, "a culture of experimentation" became a political goal in its own right.

As mentioned above, the programme specifically took a top-down, bottom-up approach (see Figure 3.6), due to interest in both RCTs/behavioural economics and start-up-style government activities/transition thinking.

Figure 3.6. The top-down, bottom-up approach of experimental culture

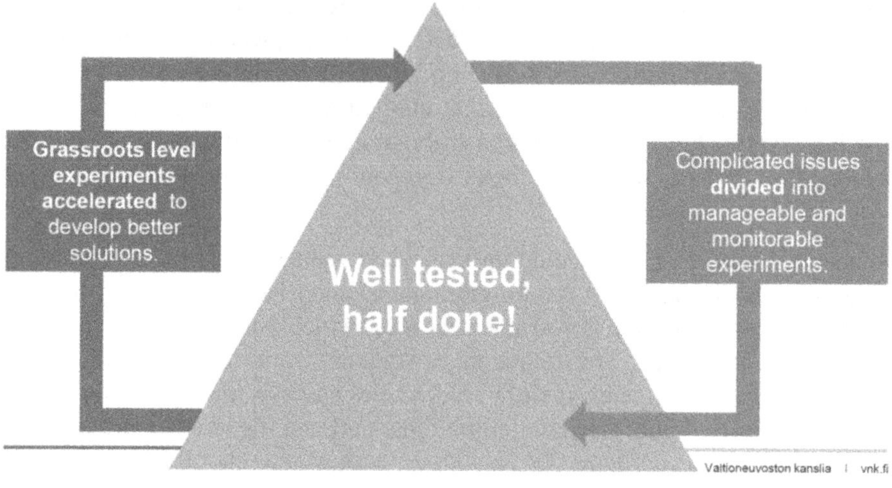

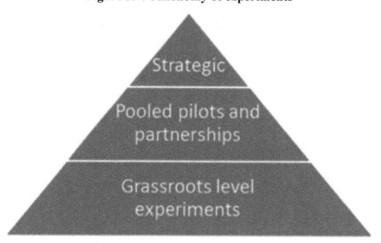

Source: Prime Minister's Office (2016).

Based on the taxonomy developed in the early phase of the Experimental Finland project by the PMO, the Experimental Finland Team engaged with three types of experiments (see Figure 3.7): strategic experiments (policy trials), pilot pools/partnerships (regionally relevant or sector-specific experiments) and grassroots-level experiments (municipalities, regions, academics, charities, etc.). The team is most heavily involved with strategic experiments, but also assists pilots and encourages grassroots-level experimentation by building networks, and facilitating and brokering experiments.

Figure 3.7. Taxonomy of experiments

Source: Experimental Finland (2016).

The Experimental Finland Team is working with a de facto "sunset clause" – they have until the end of 2017 to carry out their activities and plant seeds for further experimentation in government. There has been some discussion about extending the team's operating time, but this remains "very uncertain". They hope to achieve their goals by creating networks of experiment enthusiasts in government (including

"Kokeilukummit", the "godparents of experimentation") and building co-operation projects with other parties (e.g. polytechnics). This approach describes a top-down push for experimental culture. At the same time, the team has been asked to develop a crowdsourcing platform for grassroots experiments (Box 3.1), which tries to pull together bottom-up initiatives in the field of experimentation. This will function as a web-based toolbox and platform for experiments that will run even after the Experimental Finland Team concludes its work.

Box 3.1. A digital development platform for experimentation

In collaboration with the non-governmental organisation Demos Helsinki and the Finnish Environment Institute, the PMO's programme analysed the funding of experiments, tests and policy trials in Finland. Based on these findings, the government decided to finance a new digital funding platform for piloting and experimenting with public innovations (to be built by the Experimental Finland Team). The need for a platform/digital tool stems from the fact that experimentation at the grassroots level (municipalities, schools, etc.) is very common in Finland, but no central overview of these experiments exists. As a result, learning is coincidental and not cumulative. In its final version, the platform/digital tool should combine idea generation, posting challenges, experimentation methodologies, funding and descriptions of experiments themselves (Figure 3.8). Consequently, it should facilitate evidence-based policy making, create trust and help build a community around experiments.

Figure 3.8. Main features of the funding platform

Source: Annala (2016).

First and foremost, the platform is designed to promote useful initiatives and new practices by supporting small trials initiated by citizens. The project relies on semantic web technologies: an algorithm will gather information about experiments (in Finnish and English) from the Web. The platform will thus enable users to obtain evidence on how initiatives work in practice and help to disseminate their benefits more effectively. It will function as a toolbox, an evidence base and a crowdfunding tool for experimentation.

Ultimately, the goal is to transform the method of developing services from a top-down-dictated process to a more co-created – in some cases, even crowdsourced or crowdfunded – process for public sector innovation and, in this way, help to redefine citizen-government boundaries in the country. The government views an experimental culture as a two-way street that takes grassroots innovations and provides an avenue for acceleration through capacity building and linking innovators with reformers and sources of funding. At the same time, this culture enables countries to divide complicated issues into smaller component parts.

Box 3.1. A digital development platform for experimentation *(continued)*

The project in its entirety can be described as "lean start-up government" – the Experimental Finland Team had only six months to develop the platform. In April 2016, a political goal was set to develop a platform by the end of the year/beginning of 2017. This gave the team only a short period to develop the scope of the project. The team used the innovation funnel approach and organised four workshops to tackle the short deadlines and co-create a design for the tool. First, an open call to "godparents" was made to discuss what the platform should look like (clarification of scope). Next, they held a validation workshop with selected ICT companies to establish whether the project was possible given the timeframe. The third workshop discussed the wireframe of the platform, and the fourth explored the financing of experiments. In parallel, and as part of the procurement process, the team organised a hackathon to explore technological options for the platform/tool. While the team made progress in co-creating the platform with the experimental community, the short timeframe proved challenging. Furthermore, public procurement rules set boundaries regarding the adoption of certain solutions, which prevented the Experimental Finland Team from combining two options arrived at during the Hackathon.

Although still in its early phases, the aim of the digital platform is to highlight innovative solutions and improvements in services, promote individual initiatives and make use of citizen-driven operating practices. The platform was launched in beta and tested step-by-step during the first months of 2017. It will be launched publicly in May 2017, and be run by a private company. It will be independent from the experimental policy design programme and the Experimental Finland Team. However, without this support system it is uncertain whether the platform's information will be used effectively in government and whether the experiments will be evaluated sufficiently to have learning impacts in the public sector. The Government of Finland must therefore decide how best to ensure continued political support and buy-in after the remaining two years of its mandate, so as to ensure sustainability.

Emerging practice of experimentation

A key question arising from the experimental policy design programme is: When to use experiments? To address this point, the Experimental Finland Team adopted the NESTA typology of experiments – as outlined above. Experiments in the programme can range from rapid experimentation with no extra funding and need for randomisation to formal randomised control trials, with mixed-method design experiments (pilots, etc.) in between. In practise, however, this approach is somewhat confusing to both researchers and practitioners.

While RCTs require a lot of methodological rigour and are, thus, less well understood, grassroots experimentation is both faster and more intuitive. Due to the fast-tracked nature of the experimentation design programme, the PMO and Aalto University (with Demos Helsinki as a partner of Aalto University) are now working on a code of conduct for experiments to establish when and how to experiment (taking into account ethical concerns). "Ideally, this would have preceded the programme", however, the norms are already emerging from practise.

> *I think, if I have to generalize, the rule of thumb is that when you can without major costs carry out experiments, do, especially when you need to make sense in a complex situation, when you need rapid results. When the field is well researched already, then, the question is, why not make a decision based on the existing knowledge.*

Methodologically, experimentation should be seen as a way to move from uncertainty towards more calculable risks: making one decision and building on it with subsequent decisions. This is especially important in very complex environments. However, it is vital to keep the mandate for an experiment "clean" (and not tied directly to strategies, as the results may show that a solution should not be developed further) and the scope clear. Many interventions cannot be assessed feasibly through experimentation, and in some cases replicability is not straightforward.

Overall, five to six ministries are participating in the experimental policy design programme, and 20 to 25 experiments are ongoing. Experiments are also taking place at the municipal level (e.g. Helsinki, Rovaniemi, Eskola, Muurame and Kuopio) with the aim of increasing participation, strengthening communities, and building bridges between generations and different target groups. In addition, many other small-scale grassroots experiments are underway at smaller municipalities, such as within polytechnics.

The nature and scale of funding for experiments varies from EUR 500 to EUR 20 000 for grassroots experiments and pilots to EUR 50 000 and upwards for fully developed RCTs. Since the programme's inception, several high-level policy trials have been developed. For example, a digital municipal trial and local government trials have been initiated to curb expenditure and reduce obligations under the Minister of Local Government and Public Reforms at the Ministry of Finance. The Ministry of Education and Culture has promoted language trials, the Ministry of Social Affairs and Health is running a service voucher system trial, and the Ministry of Economic Affairs and Employment has launched regional trials in employment and business services. Nevertheless, the strategic flagship trial is the basic income experiment (see Box 3.2).

Box 3.2. Finnish basic income experiment

The public debate in Finland surrounding basic income was based on several different arguments. First of all, SITRA initiated discussions on the nature of future work, in particular: What will happen with employment after digitalisation? If full employment can no longer can be ensured and more precarious employment, stratification and unemployment emerge, what changes should the government make to the welfare system? Politicians also spoke increasingly about abolishing income traps – situations where working "does not pay" because accepting a job means a net loss in benefits and wellbeing to an individual and families. Lastly, debate surrounded the meaning of basic income and its effect on participation and belonging in society. These topics divided the nation in many ways, resulting in proponents and opponents of the basic income experiment at the political level.

The debate culminated with explicit mention of a basic income pilot as a key project of Prime Minister Juha Sipilä's government programme (29 May 2015). Within the centre-right coalition government, the main supporter of the basic income experiment was the Centre Party (Juha Sipilä's party), while other coalition partners were more sceptical (Kalliomaa-Puha, Tuovinen and Kangas, 2016). The government reserved EUR 20 million for the experiment and decided that the social transfers could be used to finance the experiment. Accordingly, unemployment benefits could be used as "basic income" in the experiment to create a much larger sample than the EUR 20 million would allow.

As part of the government's analysis and research plan for 2015, a tender was organised to create a plan for organising the experiment. A multi-disciplinary consortium led by the Social Insurance Institution (KELA) was chosen to carry out planning of the experiment, and the analysis started in September 2015. The consortium proceeded to evaluate four different models (with additional sub-models) of basic income: full basic income, partial basic income, negative income tax and other possible experiments (e.g. participation income).

Box 3.2. Finnish basic income experiment *(continued)*

The timeframe for the analysis was very tight, as the government insisted that the experiment had to be carried out during the period 2017-2018, as a general election is set for 2019. The KELA-led consortium simulated many models with different levels of basic income and flat rate taxes for basic income, and released its preliminary report – with ambitious goals for the experiment – at the end of March 2016. It included a study design for the government.[10]

However, other factors started to influence the study design. First of all, the KELA-led consortium and the Ministry of Social Affairs and Health anticipated that the Constitutional Law Committee would raise the "equal treatment" principle in Parliament once the legal changes for the experiment were enacted. Thus, every effort was made to minimise the "discrimination" of participants. This meant that different amounts of basic income could not be tested. Instead, the amounts were downscaled to equal the net level of unemployment benefits (EUR 560 per month). As one observer noted, the "baseline somehow became the ceiling".

Secondly, with limited funding available, it was clear that a full-fledged representative RCT was not possible. Within the established fiscal boundaries, the basic income experiment would be limited to unemployed people. Accordingly, the final design selected a random sample of 2 000 persons, aged between 25 and 58, who currently receive unemployment benefits from KELA. The treatment group will continue to receive their benefit of EUR 560 per month and, once employed, will keep receiving the EURO 560 per month tax free in addition to their wage. If no-one from the treatment group is employed during the experiment, the experiment's costs will amount to zero.

Thirdly, the tight schedule coupled with the need to change regulations to facilitate the experiment, and build an ICT platform to administer the benefits, meant that the experiment had to be kept as simple as possible. Stating that "it is impossible to change the tax law so quickly" for the experiment's benefit, the tax authorities simply declared that basic income would not be subject to tax nor would negative income tax be tested. The KELA-led consortium raised the issue of timing and the changes needed to make a fully representative trial possible, however the government was adamant: the experiment had to start in 2017, as "the political will was stronger".

> Sometimes it felt like we were in the middle of the reformation. Like
> Marin Luther said: here I stand, I can do no other.

As a consequence of the above, the final study design was the result of many compromises.

What was surprising to the experts involved was the lack of knowledge within the public sector regarding robust randomised control trials and the level of preparation required. Regardless, the bill was handed to Parliament in August 2016 and the study design was accepted by the Constitutional Law Committee. The law was passed and came into force on 29 December 2016, three days before the first money was paid out.

The team administrating the experiment is hopeful that the trial will function as a starting point, and that the framework will be expanded in 2018 to allow experiments with negative income tax and other forms and levels of basic income to be conducted (Kangas et al., 2017). This, however, will require fiscal and legislative changes to be made during 2017.

However, the association with Sipilä's government has raised concerns that experimentation will cease after the next elections. The new government coalition of 2019 will likely be the deciding factor. Regardless of the results of the actual experiment, sceptics will be able to use this moment to make their case. Even if the experiment is successful, critics might say that the downscaled experiment is not representative or is biased.

Box 3.2. Finnish basic income experiment *(continued)*

I think everyone's expectations were so high with the basic income experiment that when they actually saw the design of the experiment, they were really disappointed; it didn't resemble the initial model and all the aspects of basic income it was supposed to cover. So, there has been a lot of nagging connected to the experiment.

Nevertheless, the experts and academics involved are highly hopeful that robust trials of this kind will continue. By now, the government is also creating a "pilot" narrative surrounding the experiment.

There are sweeping evaluations of experiments, but you cannot compare an experiment which will affect a sector with billions of euros at stake, to other experiments.

The positioning of the basic income experiment as the flagship of the experimental policy design programme was, overall, negatively perceived by the officials interviewed for this case study. It has become the focus point of experimentation and the basic income story has garnered a lot of media attention, both in Finland and outside the country. As a highly politicised topic, its success or failure has the potential to shadow or eclipse the whole experimental policy design programme. Many experiments deliver mixed results, especially in the social context where problems are complex. Thus, the results of an experiment are subject to political or ideological framing.

Success can in many cases become a political issue. Even if we would want, as researchers, to make decisions always based on evidence, this is not the reality.

Hence, in practice experiments may be used as vessels to introduce topics into the political agenda (having robust evidence makes it easier and safer for politicians to move forwards). However, there is a danger that "bad experiments" will be utilised as a means to remove issues from the political agenda. With regard to the basic income experiment, one expert involved in the programme commented: "it will probably not kill the bottom-up experiments, but it can affect the bigger policy trials".

Impact and effects

The effects of the experimental policy design programme are unclear at this stage – it is too early to say. As one participant noted, "We are hopeful that more forward-thinking organizations will carry the approach forward, so, eventually the majority will adopt the model." Nevertheless, the feeling inside the PMO is that "it has changed the way we think about steering". Furthermore, other projects – such as SITRA's Ratkaisu 100 programme for experiments and concrete solutions connected to Finland's 100-year anniversary – underline the broader emergence of an experimental culture. Nevertheless, ministries are autonomous by nature and the PMO cannot force public organisations to experiment: "There is no way one minister can make all the decisions; it is cumulative." Some public offices are more supportive of experimentation; for example, the Ministry of Transport and Communications, which has an engineering-based practice base and, thus, less contact with citizens and their direct benefits, is very progressive.

With regard to success factors, participants made the following observations:

I would like to see five experiments go well, and then there would be some evidence about the process, some learning already.

It is not ready at the moment, but maybe in a year's time I can say yes. However, cultural change takes about seven to eight years.

Regardless, the mid-term government programme review will take place soon, and the main concern is whether the government has achieved its objectives. The review will involve a self-assessment of the PMO and ministries to find out what the experiments have accomplished in early 2017. It will conclude with a government strategy session where a political decision will be made: "Probably the political objectives may not change, but the tools of achieving them might."

The different types of experiments have led to a general consensus that simpler, bottom-up experiments are easier – "intuitive in a way, [they] just need a bit of working on the attitude of people". Conversely, bigger, more robust experiments requiring randomisation are much more difficult, as they require solid methodological skills to counter major biases, which public servants do not generally possess. Initial feedback from government seems to favour concentrating on "low hanging fruits" – in other words, simpler experiments that should produce quick returns and provide proof of concept. This may be perceived as downgrading the initiative, however it is important to demonstrate elements of success and provide measurable outcomes to legitimise the work.

What will happen after the current government reaches the end of its term? Are the seeds of experimentation rooted deeply enough in the system to become independent of political parties? It is too early to answer. While the basic income experiment is heavily associated with one party, the whole programme is not perceived directly as part of a political agenda. However, politicians also want to initiate new reform programmes associated with themselves – "everybody wants to put their own label on things" – which may affect the future survival of the programme.

The main challenges the experimental policy design programme will encounter in the future are likely connected to the equity principle and ethics, legislative differences among sectors, and generalisation and fear of wrong estimates regarding the costs involved. Experiments place people into different groups, categories which violate the equality principle that dominates most legal discussions. This may become an issue for public debate similarly to the "lottery winners" of the basic income experiment. Furthermore, such contextual factors sank RCTs in the 1970s. When experiments work in one context, this does not imply that they will work in another. This is the main critique of experiments: lack of external validity. Furthermore, many small-scale experiments and bigger RCTs are not scaled up because of fear of incorrect cost estimates. In many ways, this concern also characterised the basic income debate. As one expert asked, "What happens if this is a success? There should be a plan already."

A systems approach to reshaping an organisation's purpose and working methods: child protection services in the Netherlands

Summary

CYPSA (*Jeugdbescherming Regio Amsterdam*) is a regional Dutch organisation certified to provide Child and Youth Protection Services in the Amsterdam area. Since 2008, the organisation has worked to redefine its purpose and working methods through the "Vanguard Method", a systems thinking approach based on the "check-plan-do" cycle. As a result, the organisation adopted a new mission for its activities entitled "Every Child Safe, Forever", and redesigned its entire whole system to fulfil that purpose and ensure it had a meaningful impact. CYPSA understood that guaranteeing children's safety required changing complex family dynamics and, thus, adopted a new way of working with families that involved everybody together in the same room.

Context

In 2008, CYPSA was responsible for around 10 000 children at risk who were looked after by approximately 600 staff. The children were referred to the service by teachers, police officers, doctors or other professionals who detected signs of potential abuse or neglect. In some cases, parents accepted the involvement of the organisation voluntarily, while in others a court order was granted for an intervention if the investigation council deemed it necessary. Children also came into contact with CYPSA through parole services if a court ordered a suspended sentence for an offence. In each case, a range of welfare organisations could provide additional services to the children and families involved (e.g. foster care homes, mental health services, parental support groups, etc.). At the time the change was initiated, CYPSA was working with three different services – voluntary care, state-mandated care and parole services – and the organisation was structured and organised accordingly. This resulted in fragmented service provision, as services were organised around administrative silos.

The legal provisions underpinning the system did not permit the sharing of files between case workers from the three different groups. As a result, whenever a child was moved from one service to another (e.g. from voluntary care to parole), evaluation of their needs had to start all over again. Furthermore, the somewhat different client group profiles of the three silos disrupted collaboration among care workers, resulting in comments such as "parole doesn't do babies". The "silo" approach was reflected in the facilities of the organisation ranging from physical infrastructure to the IT system. Consequently, case workers had very different working methods and limitations to working with children: for example, parole services were limited by the time they were given, voluntary cases were bound by the terms of voluntary engagement and high caseloads, and state-mandated care by court orders lasted longer. Furthermore, in cases with multiple children in a family, each child was followed by a different case worker. Thus, it was not uncommon for families to work with a range of workers – in some cases amounting to over 20 different individuals from CYPSA over the years.

As a result of its highly bureaucratised system, CYPSA had an "infinite and costly cycle of micro-management", while "case workers did not always know how to react to signals that children were not safe". The paperwork connected to cases was immense: case workers had to complete over 20 different forms per child: "most of the day went to filling out documents" and many case reports were "more than a hundred pages long." On average, case workers spent 16 hours per week reporting on cases, rather than working with families. Additionally, the reporting system concentrated on measures related to quantity (e.g. number of caseloads, number of requests, number of kids in special care, kids flowing in and out, number of complaints, number of safety measures, number of plans, etc.), rather than on measures related to the effectiveness of interventions on children's safety. At any one time, a social worker would be responsible for around 60 children, a court ordered guardian for 18 children and a parole officer for 22 children.

Extensive paperwork and protocols were used as a means to avoid taking responsibility. People were "busy defending [their] own position, not creating value to the clients". Demonstrating that protocols were followed was sufficient to say "we did everything we could" – this, in turn, justified action (the choice of services the children were sent to) and the cleaning of caseloads. However, there was no way to prove that case workers actually contacted families or if they were reached, because no functioning follow-up system existed.

> *We were filling out these reports, calling families ... then, when parents complained ... we had proof that we had done something. We thought that this model was keeping us safe, but that wasn't real.*

All in all, the system was characterised by a variety of incompatible objectives tied to different service providers and organisations. The existence of service silos meant that different CYPSA case workers were "stereotyping problems", and consequently treating the symptoms of children at risk and not the underlying causes. Thus, short-term solutions prevailed and the organisation concentrated on "quick wins" (i.e. allocating children to services, but not verifying their wellbeing).

By 2008, the organisation was in crisis and was put under heightened supervision. The efforts required to maintain the micro-management system meant that CYPSA was facing financial bankruptcy: "after an audit the inspection found that we were out of money". However, there was little understanding in the public sector system as to what this meant. Internally, the vice-directors felt that the CEO was not fulfilling the mission of the organisation and lacked the motivation to do things differently. The directors communicated this lack of confidence to the CEO and the board. The board initially sided with the CEO and an interim director was fired, however the other directors stood their ground. Finally, the municipality exerted pressure on the board of commissioners, which resulted in the resignation of the CEO.

An intermediary CEO took control of the budget and managed to get the organisation back on track financially. In 2009, a new CEO was appointed with a background in local politics and little prior experience in child protection services. He started by gathering ideas from inside and outside the organisation on how to effect change and make the system functional again. As one observer noted, "He was open to a lot of ideas on how the organization could be changed." During this time, the CEO and the directors opened a dialogue within the employees and asked them to state explicitly the purpose of the organisation: "Why are we here? What is the problem? Why are we in this crisis?" A lot of different opinions emerged, but discussions became more focused during the process. While the nature of the discussion was largely horizontal, the reform itself was instigated from the top down by the leadership.

> *The directors really knew where they wanted to go, but they gave us the space to go through it as if it was our own process. The expectation was that we would come to see the same things that they had seen.*

The leaders opened up the discussion to staff in the hope that they would come to the conclusion the directors had already reached: that the primary objective of the organisation was looking after the children in its care. While other issues surfaced during the debates, the central issue prevailed – the organisation was not keeping children safe. This led to a bottom-up visioning process, which helped to create a new shared mission for the organisation: "Every Child Safe, Forever".[11] Based on these discussions the organisation assembled a five-year plan of change. CYPSA's leadership was open to restructuring the whole organisation, and accordingly, a programme was set up focusing on three major elements: case management methodology, development/learning and a professional working environment.

The leadership began by consulting the evidence base (the available research on child safety) and asking: How do we do this – how do we make children safe? Agreement was reached that a systems approach was needed and should focus on relationships and building a family plan. Fortunately, a family-based methodology already existed – Functional Family Parole and Probation (FFP) (Alexander and Koop, 2008) – developed for juvenile probation. In addition, the organisation was already experimenting with FFP in parole services. This working method is based on an evidence-based model of case management. It relies on family engagement and strength-based care – family as a system to tackle a child's safety – with "the whole system in one room". The core idea is to protect the child throughout changing family patterns. In 2010, the organisation started to develop an Intensive Family Case Management (IFCM) system with one case manager as a central contact for the family and care providers, and weekly multi-disciplinary team meetings (MDTMs) to share experiences.

The key question was how to shift the whole system to a totally new way of working. CYPSA already had experience with a systems thinking approach. In 2008, the organisation had used a Vanguard consultant to implement a change process in the youth parole services. The method was based on John Seddon's "check-plan-do" framework of systems change, described earlier in this report. However, the project was deemed a failure – it only dealt with one silo within the organisation and there was no acceptable evaluation or measurement system to back up the changes. As a result, the parole workers failed to perceive the impact of the change. The project did not succeed due to a combination of short implementation times – the project lasted 12 weeks with the initial "check" lasting only a week – and lack of involvement on the part of operational managers at CYPSA. As one participant noted, "The experiment was too isolated from the whole organisation, from the broader context." However, the method was deemed a success: "The project didn't succeed, but the directors thought that it was good enough to try it on the whole organization." Based on the experience, there was an understanding among the directors that you could not effect change – however, well-designed the process – unless you changed the overall system.

While the organisation still had a "change fund", this was not sufficient to kick-start the process nor carry it out in full. Accordingly, the leadership sent a social business case proposal to the municipality outlining the potential to "do a better job". The Ministry of Justice, to whom the organisation reported to at the time, was also tapped for money: "The CEO's connections in politics were very good; he was good at getting into the agendas of the people and putting our thoughts into the words of politicians." The seriousness of the situation was thus made clear to politicians:

We said that we couldn't do things in the old way anymore, and if we didn't have funds, then children had to go on a waiting list until we implemented the change. That is quite a nasty political statement. Then we told all the stories of these children to the politicians.

It took a while to assemble the funding required, but in the end the organisation drew EUR 1.5 million from its own funds and received EUR 1.5 million from the Ministry and EUR 1 million from the municipality. Once the resources were in place the change process was initiated.

One additional factor affecting the change process was that CYPSA, like the rest of the child protection service providers in the Netherlands, was expecting a wider reform of the system and the passing of a new youth care law. The government had planned a change in youth care responsibilities in 2015, with child protection services due to be moved from the central government (Ministry) to the municipal level. This change meant that CYPSA would be allocated the most difficult cases with easier cases going to local services. The quality of service therefore had to increase because the new client base would need more help.

Initiating a process of systems change

Renewal of the organisation commenced in 2010 with a change in team managers. The directors of CYPSA wanted to be sure that the leaders shared the newly defined purpose of the organisation. Team managers had to reapply for their jobs via a process involving external experts well acquainted with the organisation. Five team managers left the organisation during this process. Although there was resistance to change, the leadership adhered to the plan and held frequent discussions with the parties involved. As a result of these debates the employees engaged in the process, which they associated with management, but identified with the change themselves.

> *First there was quite a lot of resistance to change. It is just another change and everybody was tired of the constant changes. That is the thing behind the fundamental change – everybody felt and saw the change, it came from the bottom up, not top down.*

In 2011, a more systematic change process was initiated to lead the whole organisation towards new working methods. The Vanguard consultant guided a development team of ten case managers and two team managers through the process of "check-plan-do". The consultant had exceptionally good leadership skills and believed in the change process: "You need one person to light the fire, there probably is no other way." The first group was carefully selected: the top leadership of CYPSA looked for specific traits including a willingness to question the status quo.[12] Around 20 people were asked to make presentations to the selection committee; they were asked to reflect on their own actions, and their ability to perform in front of a group, and their creativity was evaluated. The final group consisted of people of varying ages coming from different backgrounds; however, due to the gendered nature of social work nine of the core team of ten were women.

The organisation's leadership gave the initial development team "carte blanche" in their approach. The directors were invited into the process quite often – "we didn't push, we let them pull" – to explain their vision of the process and the overall system, and to help the consultant. People initially found it difficult to think outside their domain, so some guidelines were set: there needed to be one work process for the whole organisation, one methodology (end of silos) and the team had to consider FFP as a working method. The main idea was that families would receive the same service to ensure their children's safety (e.g. case workers would remain with families for six to nine months) regardless of how they initially came into contact with the organisation – voluntarily, by court order or through parole. Beyond these guidelines, the team was free to experiment. The development team worked together for three months and conducted a full "check-plan-do."

The "check phase" evaluated current activities and imposed a sense of urgency. The team worked through 60 case files to establish which activities added value and which did not. In 53 out of 60 cases, the family situation had not improved or had worsened because of the intervention. This realisation was "truly eye-opening" and "depressing", and underlined the lack of focus at the heart of the organisation. The change process therefore aimed to take people out of their comfort zones and get them to ask themselves questions such as: How do I do my job? How should I do it? How far I am from doing it successfully? However, "we had to be clear that it is not an individual failure, but the system's conditions [that produced] this result." The safety of the children needed to be put first and, to achieve that, new family patterns had to be created to guarantee their safety. This created a common, shared vision of the system: "this is my goal, this is my client". The team them analysed the process from the clients' point of view. The findings of the process are illustrated in Figure 3.9.

Figure 3.9. The findings of the check phase

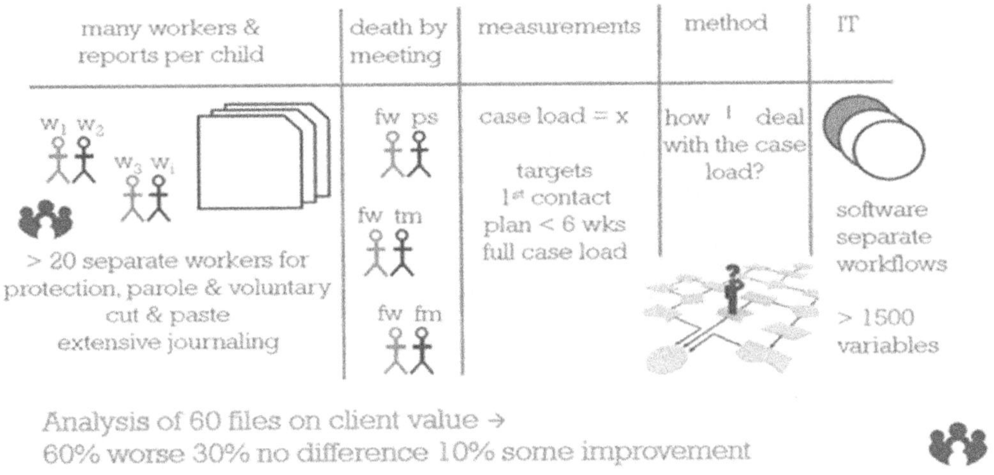

many workers & reports per child	death by meeting	measurements	method	IT
w_1 w_2 w_3 w_4 > 20 separate workers for protection, parole & voluntary cut & paste extensive journaling	fw ps fw tm fw fm	case load = x targets 1st contact plan < 6 wks full case load	how I deal with the case load?	software separate workflows > 1500 variables

Analysis of 60 files on client value →
60% worse 30% no difference 10% some improvement

Source: Wauters and Dinkgreve (2016).

During the subsequent "plan" phase the development team created a vision for the organisation. This was not an easy process: "It was difficult sometimes to comment on [the] processes – say that something was done wrong, talk back to the director and say that you have to do this, so we can move forward." Nevertheless, the process "helped to understand that the only one that can change the system is you yourself. You just need the balls to talk back to the directors."

The purpose of the system was revisited in order to focus on the most important steps and identify "waste" in the system. Figure 3.10 summarises the findings of the "plan phase".

Figure 3.10. The findings of the plan phase

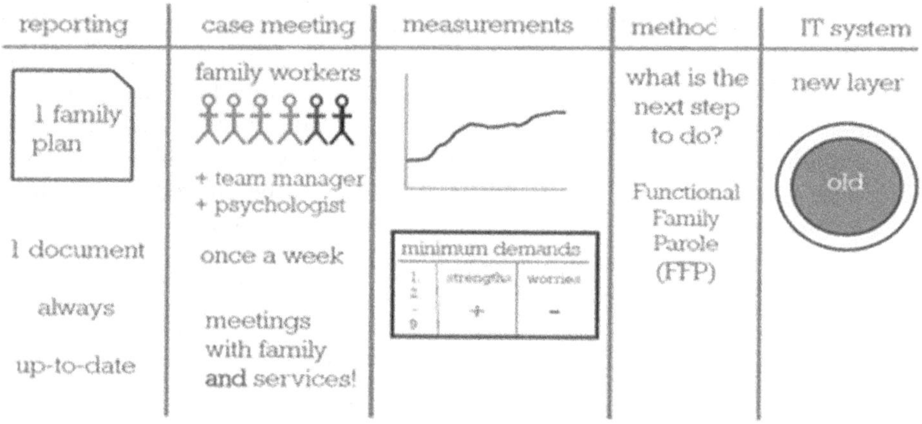

reporting	case meeting	measurements	method	IT system

Source: Wauters and Dinkgreve (2016).

The team elaborated a "one family, one plan, one worker, one method" approach based on the FFP methodology. First and foremost, the new working method would bring the whole system together in one room – parents, children, grandparents, neighbours, teachers and so on. This helps to address and remove the "privacy issue". An engagement with a family would now involve three phases: (i) engage and motivate, (ii) support and monitor, and (iii) generalisation.

A purpose-driven approach was also adopted – "if you know the strengths of the family, then you know which strings to pull to help". The change consisted of four main elements:

- from protection-oriented to strength-based care

- from problem-driven to pattern-oriented care

- from standardised to tailor-made care

- from process-oriented to purpose-driven care (Van Veelen et al., 2017).

This resulted in the following process:

In the first 6-12 weeks, meetings are held with the family as often as necessary. The intention is to build trust, so while the causes of the safety issues are addressed, the case worker does not rub the families' nose in all of their problems all the time. The basic assumption is that families have a noble intent but that for some reason they are not living up to this. Case workers look for strengths in the family that they can build on. They do not utter judgement and need to respect the ways of the family. But it is paramount that the safety of the child is discussed and if they refuse to do that, then this constitutes an issue that must be addressed. The case worker does this by increasing the families' insight in the harm that children are exposed to (Wauters and Dinkgreve, 2016).

In addition, the process would guarantee a smooth transition for families in the event that a case worker changed. In this situation, a case worker would identify and meet with their counterpart to hand over a case. As a result, each team manager now coaches two to three teams comprising on average seven case workers, one senior case worker (supervisor) and a psychologist (teams previously consisted of 20 people). Teams are, thus, to an extent autonomous, so that in principle they have at their disposal all the required skills and can accomplish everything needed to achieve their purpose. However, personal characteristics also play a key role as it is very important to find a good match between the case worker and family.

The first development team was happy with the process, with one participant noting, "I am spoiled for the rest of my life, because it was an ideal way of changing the system". Training from the Vanguard consultant enabled them to act as "tour guides" for the rest of the teams, who were to be introduced to the new working method with the aim of guiding the rest of the organisation in different cohorts through the check-plan-do phase.

In December 2011, a pilot was initiated with six teams (five to seven case managers, one psychologist and one team manager). Following its success, approximately 20 remaining teams were guided through a condensed "check-plan-do" process in three cohorts. The teams received three weeks off from work while other workers in the organisation took over their caseloads. During the first week they passed through the "check" and "plan" phases. This involved analysing their present way of working, existing case files and value demand, and resulted in the realisation that they were not doing their job to keep children safe. This resulted in depression and a sense of urgency. As one interviewee noted, "Everybody needs a personal crisis."

During the second and third week, old files were transferred to the new ICT system which supports family work. In the ten weeks that followed the teams passed through the "do" phase. After the initial "check" week, the "tour guides" stayed with the teams for three months to help them shape their working methods. The teams needed to learn how to write about families in a different way, using a one-page word document that is succinct and clear about priorities. This would be used for weekly meetings to ensure that all participants had the most important pieces of information. For many this proved difficult and the "tour guides" needed to have one-on-one conversations with several team members. Not everyone was capable of switching to this approach: "People were on board in the beginning [and] understood the need to change in the moment … but were unable to follow through … We only later noticed that." A complete "rolling in"[13] took a full quarter.

The whole process with different cohorts lasted more than a year and finished in June 2013. However, in reality, it took more than three years to guide the whole organisation – comprising approximately 40 teams (finishing with the facility teams) – through the change process. Every round ended with a session of discussion, evaluation and feedback. The sequencing of these teams was determined by the closure of their offices, so as to ensure that the new teams could start in new offices once the three-week period was completed. This meant that the change process was accompanied by a physical change that was visible to people. However, there was some doubt about the wisdom of planning the change process and the cohorts alongside office closures, with some suggesting that maybe teams consisting of volunteers should have been preferred.

The facilities were designed in line with the new working methods. They included a family-based filing option in the IT system, open offices with no assigned places, company catering with former clients as employees, and pictures of former clients and mission statements on walls, all of which was designed to remind workers of their mission to keep children safe (see Figure 3.11). As one employee noted: "Everything from the colour of the walls and carpets on the floors is considered from the perspective of how does this help us keep children safe", while another described the new emphasis on quality and purpose as: "Less, but better coffee."

Figure 3.11. Examples of new facilities

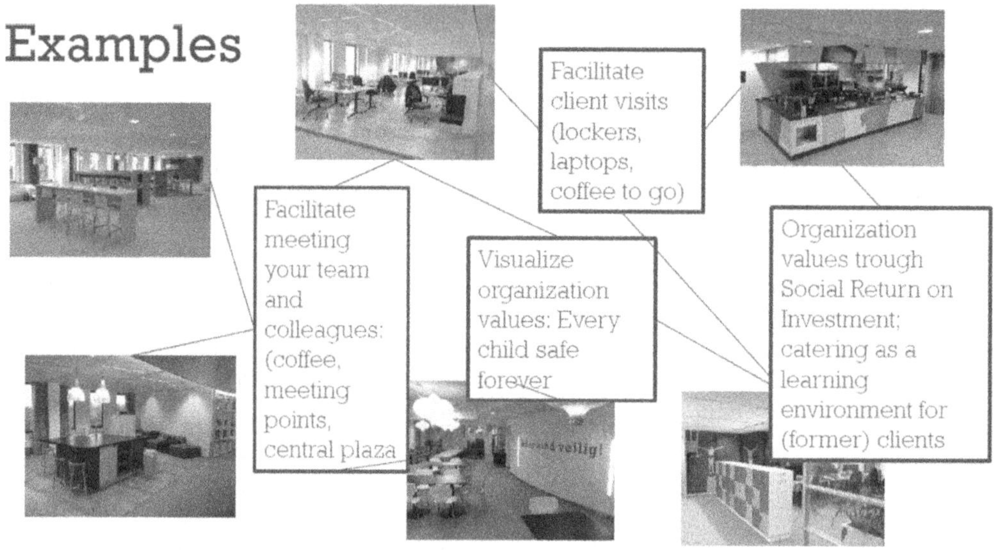

Source: Dinkgreve (2016).

The idea was that case managers should spend 80% of their time outside the office (instead of behind the desk). Accordingly, they were supplied with laptops, smartphones with mobile data connections, public transport cards, access to shared/public car parks and so on. In retrospect, all changes to facilities in support of the new system should have made right away. For example, the option to classify data according to families and not individual children was layered on top of an existing IT system in the hope that a new system would be designed after. Thus, the system did not mirror the primary work process – how the organisation really wanted to work – and CYPSA is still working on the new platform. As one respondent stated, "We should have gone for a new IT process from the start." At this level of transformation piecemeal changes do not work.

Support services were outsourced to maintain flexibility and the organisation was consolidated in one office, which is now used mostly by administration and for weekly team meetings.

Before there were seven different locations [There was] no policy [on] how to distribute people in the rooms, everybody was at their offices, behind their desks. Everything was designed to facilitate paperwork. People were asking for more drawer space just to store all the paper.

In general, facility managers need to know more about the activities:

We need to continuously go through the "check" phase. Are we really helping people and helping to keep children safe? It can be quite annoying to people ... but we need to know more about the work to actually help them. Being continually conscious of this is still difficult.

The change, however, created new challenges and issues within the system, as problems tied to existing capabilities and staff characteristics started to emerge. The general staff did not have to reapply for their jobs but the "normal annual performance cycle did show that only 50% of staff performed according to [the new] expectations"

(Wauters and Dinkgreve, 2016). The employees were given two years to improve their performance in line with these expectations or were asked to leave. The changes showed that the overall "IQ of the organization needed to go up". This was not an easy process for team managers and was not without personal hardship:

> *You had to have really clear conversations with people. It wasn't about them as people, you still feel loyal to the person... they just weren't capable of working in the new system. People had a lot of problems with feeling safe within the organization.*

> *People get very personal, teams have worked together for a long time, but when co-workers see what is going on in actual families, they stop sheltering their colleagues and understand why we needed to part ways.*

There were several waves of leavers: after the change approximately 40% of the workforce left; and another group of people left in 2015 when the employment market improved following the economic crisis. "People were not right for the job." In essence, this meant a five-year process of employee removal. Still, the annual turnover rate remained at approximately 20%.

> *Maybe it was too much responsibility in too short of a time, especially for new people. How to protect the new case workers? There are some mindfulness and vitality trainings, but the work is very demanding.*

Meaningful measurement became a core issue within the office. If an organisation is "living a purpose" then that needs to be measured. Thus, CYPSA began to measure "acute child safety" by simply rating the situation using a score from 0 to 10, where a 5 is insufficient and a 6 is just acceptable (see Figure 3.12). Statistical process charts were produced to measure how long it takes to complete a phase of work. Other key management information includes capacity planning (e.g. how many families are presently in a specific phase of the process). In addition, teams now conduct an internal peer-to-peer audit once a year. This is not to enforce top-down control, but ownership.

Figure 3.12. Acute child safety

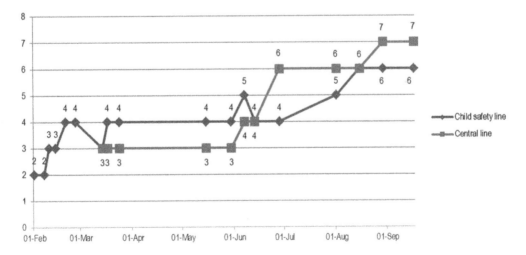

Source: Based on Dinkgreve 2016.

The main feedback loop is created through three-hour weekly team meetings – MDTMs. Other meetings were cut to ensure everyone was on the same page and to enable those involved to review family plans, learn and reflect together. Accordingly, information is shared and families are no longer considered "clients of individuals, but clients of the organization." Each weekly meeting covers 8 to 20 cases. Previously, team managers attended up to 20 meetings per week, with case workers averaging 5-6 meetings. The MDTMs also count towards a case worker's license registration.

The organisation remains dependent on services from other organisations (e.g. foster homes, mental health services, etc.) that have not undergone systems change or prioritised their activities – and are likely facing financial pressures. To this end, CYPSA's leadership designed a specific issue management protocol. If an obstacle cannot be resolved at a lower level, it is referred upwards and undergoes a critical review. This covers issues linked to cooperation with partners, where the CEO might have to step in and negotiate at a higher level.

Impact and effects

The results of systems change at CYPSA were impressive. Employee satisfaction with working conditions grew from 6.3 to 7.5 (6.9 is the national average for similar organisations) and the total annual costs of facilities (including IT) reduced by 32% (Dinkgreve, (2016). Costs per user reduced by 22% (the cost of taking care of an entire family in 2014 was only marginally higher than taking care of one child in 2011), while the quality of service increased. Client satisfaction rose from 5.8 to 7.5 on an 11-point scale (Wauters and Dinkgreve, 2016). As a result, the change produced a return on the initial investment within 1.5 years. Furthermore, fewer referrals to specialist services were required and the courts were less involved in compelling parents to cooperate with the service (see Figure 3.13). Use of legal instruments reduced by 60% and instances of legal guardianship by a case worker decreased by 16% (while it rose nationally by 3%) (ibid). The leadership acknowledged that in the best-case scenario there would be zero court referrals: "Our goal is to have no court-based emergency placement; our purpose is to be non-existent and the children safe at the end of the line."

Figure 3.13. Reduction in court measures

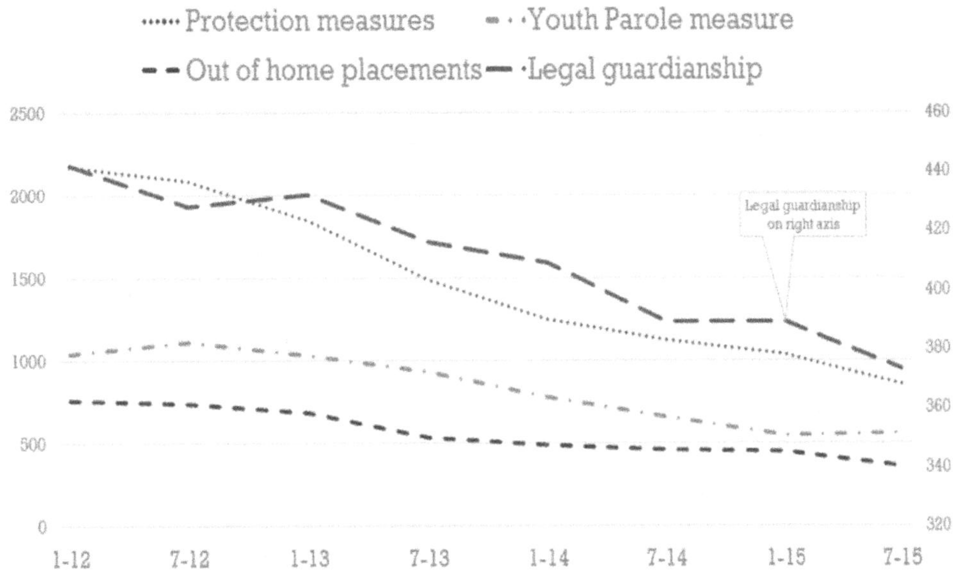

····· Protection measures ▪·· Youth Parole measure ▬ ▬ Out of home placements ▬ ·Legal guardianship

Source: Dinkgreve (2016).

Evaluation and comparisons with other service providers in the Netherlands remain quite difficult, however, as comparisons are not done in a meaningful way:

Evaluation is quite difficult. We can evaluate if we are doing a better job, but to compare with before... we have changed so much. We are not representative of the rest of the country anymore; the starting point is so different.

Everybody in Holland is at the moment reducing measures like court cases, but as our measures are so much lower compared to others; we don't have anywhere to go. But we are still told to reduce. We are so ahead of the game – but still compared to the game.

While the systems change was impressive, it was not without its challenges. The broader system has not changed and some bureaucratic requirements have remained. For example, should case workers have separate evaluation sessions for their license if these already form part of their weekly MDTMs? While this issue was resolved, a recent audit uncovered the fact that a questionnaire required by law was not used by most case workers. The questionnaire does not benefit the core mission of keeping children safe, but its lack of use can affect CYPSA's license.

The last audit showed that in connection to parole a specific questionnaire is not done. It is really useless, but it is a legal obligation and this might make problems for our license.

The organisation through the change has become so purpose-driven that there is a risk that the broader accountability system – which has not changed – will be forgotten, and this can hurt the organisation in the long run.

We have to become better at keeping our promises. If we say that we are going to do something then we should do it, even if it doesn't make directly sense with our mission.

They say that we are best in the country,[14] you are really doing a good job. But you also need to stick to the regulatory agreements, otherwise they will take our license away. It is very frustrating, but it also shows that [systems change] is a little bit illusionary ... we exist in a larger context.

In addition to the above, the capacity of CYPSA to guarantee a quality service on a continuous basis poses a major challenge. The organisation's resources during the change were stretched quite thin.

The biggest challenges with systems change are money and time. You need money to create time to implement the changes. Later on, you need endurance to stick to the change.

The most difficult part was that the organization had a workload, still has a workload and had a workload during the change process. However, everybody needs to have time to go through the process. It is still a struggle to find time for development.

However, CYPSA enjoyed quite stable leadership during the change process. While the CEO left in 2015, two of the directors remained: "It is a big city; things don't change so fast here." But with the child protection system reform in 2015, work became tougher. CYPSA now takes the most difficult cases in the region – such as multi-problem families – while simpler case go to local services. This means that turnover and sick leave are high. While caseloads went down (now at 10-14 families, compared to 22 parole, 18 youth and 60 voluntary workers before the change), these numbers went up. In addition, the content and expectation of results have changed. CYPSA insists on tailor-made care programmes, rather than ready-made – "this is the best we can offer" – solutions. Thus, there are long waiting lists,[15] which present both a moral and a political problem to the organisation:

Waiting lists in our area are really politically incorrect. Our alderman gets bullied a lot in the newspapers about this.

There is a moral dilemma: can you put children in these circumstances on a waiting list. We have a responsibility to the families.

Due to the changing nature of the work – strength-based, problem-driven, tailor-made, purpose-driven care – finding the right people to do the job has become a crucial issue. "We need team managers and case workers who are purpose living." The requirement for different kinds of people necessitates a fundamental change in the recruitment and training system of the organisation. The strength-based system means ensuring that workers do not "take over" families.

Families get under yours skin; you can see terrible things, but you need to stand by and not take over. Most social workers want to take over and lead in such situations.

We need people that want to save the world, but also know how to shut the door behind the work when they go home. It is very difficult to save people; you need to be happy with little things, little improvements.

CYPSA devised a new recruitment procedure in 2012 that combined personality assessment (empathy, self-reflection, support without taking over, ability to direct/authority, orderly, collaborative, etc.) with an IQ test. Regardless, the organisation still has difficulty finding the right people who also reflect the mix and diverse backgrounds of the families they deal with. Most new workers enter after experiencing the system during traineeships through school (new people join teams at CYPSA as part of a ten-month internship during the third year at university). This becomes a "recruitment floor" for the organisation, and enables people to become familiar with the working methods. High turnover rates and a lower influx of people also adds to stress – "the staff gets exhausted" – and waiting lists.

Due to the changing working method, training needs have changed drastically. In 2012-2013, the organisation started to develop a new training approach. They opted for a shift towards a more extensive programme (eight-month training programme for new workers) with more reflection. "It is needed as our working methods are not taught in school." As a result of developing these programmes, CYPSA is making a profit through its academy by training other social teams in the municipality and voluntary workers and giving courses at higher education schools and hospitals.

CYPSA is especially interested in showcasing the project and finding new ways of working to service partners. Initially the organisation was heavily focused on its internal change process and external partners were little bit side-lined:

We were very focused on our own process and we didn't involve external parties enough; only direct stakeholders. It was a bit arrogant, inflexible to later on say to external parties that we had the best solution in the world. It was not surprising that the surrounding organisations were not enthusiastic. But we are working on external engagement now. It's an ongoing process with judges, the board of child protection, external service providers and colleagues in the rest of the country.

At the same time, the organisation relies on support services (e.g. mental health workers) in order to do their job:

These families encounter a lot of complex problems coming from drug use, alcohol, mental illnesses, depression. Mental health workers tend to work with individuals, while the need would be to look at them also as parents. This is a whole new area.

This is a public value debate: What is more important, the parent or the child? Most service providers have not examined their role in this light.

At first, we were obsessed with spreading the word [and] talked about unnecessary division of labour – for example, domestic violence. But then people said, wait you are talking about my job!

Regardless, this approach has been disseminated to a degree in the Netherlands: Zeeland ran a small-scale project to test the methodology, and child protection services in the Hague are currently undergoing the same systems change process. In both cases, the same Vanguard consultant was involved in the project. However, in Zeeland the systems change failed because it was designed as a small-scale, sped-up process: "they tried to do the same in Zeeland in three months that we did in Amsterdam in three years." In the Hague, the child and youth protection organisation is of a similar size to CYPSA in Amsterdam and the process is comparable. However, you "cannot just copy it"; the process needs to be adapted to local specificities: operational managers must be more involved in directing their teams through the rolling-in process. Furthermore, the failure in Zeeland demonstrated that top management needs to back the process, and that sometimes people just do not fit: "it's also a personal thing, you need to have people on the floor who understand why the change is needed". This point highlights one of the deficiencies of the Vanguard Method: it assumes that everything revolves around the system. The personal element and the effects of organisational culture are not acknowledged.

> *What I have seen in my work is that connecting and matching the right people is really important. You need different people and different skills sets to make the change work.*

> *Vanguard was a starting point, not a perfect methodology, but it created time and space to review our actions and follow up with issues.*

On the whole, the Netherlands is open to adopting new management perspectives, but there is also a danger that the purpose behind the system will disappear.

> *The Netherland is, on the whole, curious; organisations are open to all kinds of hypes and trends every 6-12 months. From a system development perspective, this creates a lot of frustration and anger.*

> *So-called innovators are mostly warm about ideas, and not about if they work on the floor – within the system. It is not just about great ideas.*

This is the main takeaway from this case study: stability and consistency in adapting systems change is the key to successful reform.

Using systems approaches to regulate the sharing economy: Public transportation in Toronto (Canada)

Summary

Disruptive technological change and the emergence of the platform economy – specifically the sharing economy – is at the core of this case study. Technological change produces new means of providing services with new types of supply and demand that do not fit into legacy economic models regulated by government. This poses a challenge to policy while shaking up incumbent industries.

In Canada, digitalisation impacts all levels of government – city, province and federal – because policies connected to emerging fields of the sharing economy (e.g. housing and transportation bylaws, insurance, taxation, etc.) are regulated at different levels of government. This creates a problem – who has ownership over the issue? In addition, regulators needed to catch up with changing technology. In 2014, the transportation network company Uber started to operate in Toronto without specific regulatory oversight. The city had to move quickly to implement new regulation and appease the alarmed incumbent industry. In order to tackle the regulatory challenge and simultaneously preserve the beneficial aspects of a sharing economy, an independent arbiter, MaRS Solutions Lab, facilitated productive dialogue between the different stakeholders. Utilising systems thinking and design methodologies, they proposed a user-centric vision and a sharing economy city strategy for Toronto (and by extension cities across Ontario). They also helped develop new legislation that enables the city and its citizens to both regulate and benefit from new entrants that disrupt old businesses.

Context

The sharing economy became a key topic in the Canadian public sector in the early 2010s. However, corresponding demand for regulation had not yet reached critical mass and governments across Canada had adopted different trajectories in response to the sharing economy. For example, in January 2016, Edmonton became the first city in Canada to pass an Uber-friendly bylaw stating that Uber drivers could obtain a license if they had provincially approved insurance. Due to the relatively small size of the locality, the law did not catalyse similar legislation across Alberta. As one observer complained: "the problem in Canada and elsewhere are the amateur politicians. They want to put a stamp on the regulation – 'Made in City X' – while a lot might be learned by looking elsewhere". Overall, governments were slow to react, either because of attempts to produce "perfect regulation" or because of a lack of impetus.

Government had already been working to address the sharing economy, especially at the federal and provincial levels, but a push for concrete regulation had not yet materialised. In 2015, Ontario initiated their process, which involved up to seven ministries, but there was no clear leadership other than the coordination role provided by the Office of the Premier. The province did not see itself as a key actor in determining regulation – the principal issue from the perspective of the administrative authority seemed to be the regulation of appropriate insurance products. Moreover, most sharing economy issues such as labour laws and taxation are connected to municipal bylaws or federal law. Ontario's sharing economy advisory committee did prepare initial reports, but no concrete procedural recommendations. This was in part because officials struggled to articulate the exact nature of the problems and opportunities. As one official said, "we didn't know where to point our lawyers." Meanwhile, the Ontario Chamber of Commerce organised the first regional conference on the sharing economy in March 2015, which led to the publication of several reports (e.g. the Mowat report).[16]

At the federal level, a senior committee was established to identify barriers to innovation, including the sharing economy, under the heading "Are we missing the boat?" The committee consisted of an interested team of experts from across government – a tiger team – charged with considering the sharing economy and potential regulatory gaps. The team prepared an overview report entitled *Back to the Future* in February (DMCPI+, 2015). They also commissioned a second phase overview (regarding tax revenue, social/employment issues, public safety and innovation) that concluded prior to the elections in October 2015. However, the reports seemingly had only a minimal impact, in part because the principal lead, the Deputy Minister in the field of innovation, did not have direct authority over the issues in question. However, members of the tiger team would later participate in MaRS Solutions Lab workshops and contribute insights (gathered in their reports) to foundational research conducted by the MaRS team.

In the meantime, large-scale tech platforms such as Uber and AirBnB have become the poster children for the sharing economy, advancing their businesses and, in some cases, regulation forward at their own pace, while arguing that disruption was inevitable. Yet, both companies have very different strategies for dealing with regulation: Uber is generally deemed to be more aggressive, while AirBnB tries to look for ways to work with regulators. As one interviewee noted:

> *AirBnB has gotten a free pass in Toronto (while already being regulated in Vancouver with severe restrictions). The aggressive tactics of Uber really played a role in pushing the issue forward.*

Uber's more confrontational strategy placed the company at the forefront of regulators' concerns. As one official noted, "AirBnB is simply not on our radar". Furthermore, the city of Toronto struggled with being proactive in the face of new challenges, as is true for many municipalities.

Uber opened for business in Toronto in 2012, initially as a technology company dispatching rides to taxi drivers, while building up public awareness and a client base. At the time, the city of Toronto had just conducted an extensive review of taxi services – one of the largest consultations the city had ever held – but did not include car-sharing or Uber in its analysis. This reflected a lack of anticipatory systems thinking capacity among city authorities to tackling emerging issues such as disruptive technologies. The Municipal Licensing & Standards (ML&S) Division, which was responsible for the review and had administrative authority over taxis, had long operated in a traditional enforcement capacity rather than leading norm creation. For instance, ML&S's remit covers taxi licensing, but also includes pet adoption, dead animal removal and bylaw enforcement with regard to fireworks, noise complaints and garage sales. The challenges presented by car and home-sharing business platforms fell outside their realm of expertise and therefore challenged the city's organisational structure, which favoured administrative action:

> *The city has really good capacity from an engineering lens: planning subways, roads, etc. But it does not have capacity to talk about wicked problems, about geographies of neighbourhoods. There is no concrete dialogue about homeless shelters, poverty, etc.*

Traditionally, there is a time lag when dealing with problems in the public sector; but in 2014, Toronto was faced with a crisis: UberX had launched and begun operating in the city. This situation posed a whole set of new problems for the city: how to deal with and regulate a multi-national enterprise with sophisticated lobbyists and lawyers, especially in a regulatory domain where there is no easy common compromise (i.e. the city's regulatory approach would result in winners and losers). The city needed to gather intelligence about the impact of Uber's operations. This included the effect of Uber in terms of growing uncertainty in the areas of employment, economic rents, service levels, public safety and so on. However, the authorities' initial "knee-jerk" reaction was to file an injunction to prevent UberX from operating what it deemed to be an illegal business, an action supported by the taxi industry. However, the injunction was rejected by a judge who ruled that the city's bylaws did not apply to Uber's business model. Meanwhile, the new mayor of Toronto publicly expressed his support for the company, stating "Uber is here to stay", citing Toronto's role in leading urban innovation in Canada. In addition, citizens were validating UberX's value with high usage numbers and generally positive reviews. This situation placed public officials under significant pressure to take action – either to legalise or stop UberX – thus forcing the city to become a pioneer in regulating the sharing economy.

In 2015, the MaRS Solutions Lab offered to help the city prepare regulation for the sharing economy. The lab is located within the MaRS Discovery District, an urban innovation hub in Toronto that works with corporations, investors, mentors, university institutions and labs to accelerate innovation.[17] MaRS Solutions Lab received grant funding from the Government of Ontario to work on regulatory burden reduction and to help level the playing field for the sharing economy (see Box 3.3).

Box 3.3. MaRS Solutions Lab: the road to the sharing economy

In 2011, high-level political interest in cutting red tape and addressing "sticky issues" at the Ministry of Research and Innovation in the Government of Ontario was brought to the fore by a conference that included presentations about design and systems thinking from organisations such as Mindlab (Denmark) and Helsinki Design Lab (Finland). Some of those most receptive to systems thinking and design moved to Open for Business (OFB), which leads Ontario's government-wide burden reduction and service modernisation efforts (Government of Ontario, 2014). In 2012, a proposal was made to use design methodologies to cut red tape. However, lack of capacity meant that OFB had to choose whether to build capabilities in-house or support the development of capacity outside the organisation. Forward-thinking leaders among the senior political staff and at the deputy minister level recognised that systems change was necessary and that the old model of "throwing money at problems" was no longer appropriate given their complexity and the pressure on public budgets. However, there was little capacity for transformative change inside government, and fear of political interference, as well as a belief that public procurement rules would block creation of an innovation lab. Thus, the OFB concluded that it would be better to provide seed funding to MaRS Solutions Lab, a public and social innovation lab.[18]

The newly appointed director of the MaRS Solutions Lab, Joeri van den Steenhoven, had more than ten years of experience in social innovation and burden reduction in government (Kafka Brigade, Kennisland). During his work in the Netherlands, he had begun to merge design methodologies and systems thinking in order to understand problems at a systemic level, while developing solutions at the scale of products and services.

The partnership between MaRS Solutions Lab and OFB began by identifying particularly difficult policy problems on which they could collaborate. Social policy challenges such as indigenous youth and chronic health were considered, but proved too complex and mired in political conflict for the initial project of a new partnership. In addition, OFB lacked direct ownership over the issues.

Meanwhile, the lab was involved in parallel discussions regarding the challenges Uber and AirBnB posed at the municipal level. OFB's focus on burden reduction in government, reducing regulation and creating an efficient regulatory system to make the market function creatively, appeared to create a convergence of opportunities. As a result, discussions started to explore ways to ensure new market entrants played by the same rules (e.g. safety, taxes, consumer confidence, etc.). OFB also saw an opportunity to level the playing field in terms of tackling the over-regulation burdening the existing taxi industry, which struggled to innovate under numerous municipal bylaws and other legacy constraints. While many of these burdens fell outside the authority of the province, OFB nonetheless backed a grant-based project led by MaRS Solutions Lab under the auspice of burden reduction. A grant was used to avoid the de facto limitations to innovative approaches imposed by public procurement regulations. In general, OFB felt that existing government tools were not working and that new policy tools were needed. Organisations such as MaRS Solutions Lab could help compensate for these gaps until procurement and other barriers to innovation were lifted.

For MaRS Solutions Lab, the make-up of participating project stakeholders was a critical issue. The lab agreed to proceed with the project only if the city – as the "owner" of the problem – was on board. It had learned from past experience that projects do not gain traction without buy-in from the organisations directly involved – both inside and outside government. Under the best possible scenario, MaRS would function as a neutral convener between the public and private sectors and function as the glue between the various levels of government with a stake in the sharing economy.

Thus, the project started with collaboration and funding from the province and then city officials were approached to be "content" partners. As the city of Toronto lacked capacity and expertise in the domain of the sharing economy, they were delighted. As one observer shared, "I think the officials at the City of Toronto had tears in their eyes knowing that someone [MaRS Solutions Lab] was going to come in and help them tackle the issue".

MaRS Solutions Lab represented new, innovative capacity for the city, which lacked sufficient excess funds to build up policy capacity quickly to address emergent challenges. As one city official concluded, "We have a lot of money, but we don't have a lot of money". Most funding was dedicated to service provision and operations, leaving little for internal R&D around policy questions. Furthermore, MaRS Solutions Labs' ability to work with different kinds of methods and approaches was especially helpful, because regulators were unclear about the exact nature of the question they were trying to answer. They were being asked to regulate a dual disruption of an industry and a policy process. Accordingly, the city's level of uncertainty was high, as evidenced by remarks by officials:

> *If we want numbers, data crunching or confirmation of already known answers, we go to Deloitte, KPMG, etc., but here we didn't want that. This was a question where we didn't know the answer in advance.*

> *Outsourcing policy is very simple for the city, nothing really new. Outsourcing can help to bring some legitimacy to a process. However, when commissioning KPMG or Deloitte we almost always know what they will say. In this case, the response to a disruption was an opportunity to do some coherent thinking and develop solutions that are credible.*

Due to the involvement of the province and OFB, the project had a clear focus: how to make new entrants to the market play by the rules, while rebalancing regulatory burden on incumbent industries. The taxi industry was perceived to be over-regulated – taxi drivers were required to complete a 17-day training course and have CPR certification, a medical certificate, and so on – and oligopolistic with a core operating framework established decades ago. While the lab was charged with providing alternative solutions for regulators, their working premise was that they must first determine the potential benefits of the sharing economy for Toronto and its citizens, and only then set out to design a regulatory response.

Initiating a process of systems change

The lab's work started in earnest in the summer of 2015. Their brief was to identify what the sharing economy could mean for Toronto and design a new regulation system that would help the city realise those potential benefits. This approach represented a significant departure from business as usual. As one person involved shared, "Usually, politicians want regulation – it proves that they are doing something. But sometimes it is not necessary to add requirements to business and citizens." Thus, MaRS Solutions Lab needed to establish what compliance with regulation would mean for Uber, taxis, the city and its citizens.

Since its inception, MaRS Solutions Lab has experimented with its own working methodology, which has since been codified as a "Periodic Table of Systems Change". The essential premise of this methodology is a merger between design thinking and systems thinking. The periodic table provides a framework for understanding the different kinds of elements required to comprehend, navigate and intervene in complex systems. The method acknowledges that for systems to change, it is not enough to tackle policies and provide solutions; to ensure a successful process, systems thinking must also build the capacities of different stakeholders. Figure 3.14 illustrates how different stages of systems change – hypotheses, research, testing and marketing – are considered through the phases of capacity building, solution design and policy making. Working with the system means crossing each phase during the different stages of the work process, both horizontally and vertically. During the design of a systems change process, each phase requires different actions and resources. The MaRS process combines the actions outlined in the table with ethnographic research that enables the team to understand different user groups and their influence within the system.

Figure 3.14. MaRS Solutions Lab's Periodic Table of Systems Change

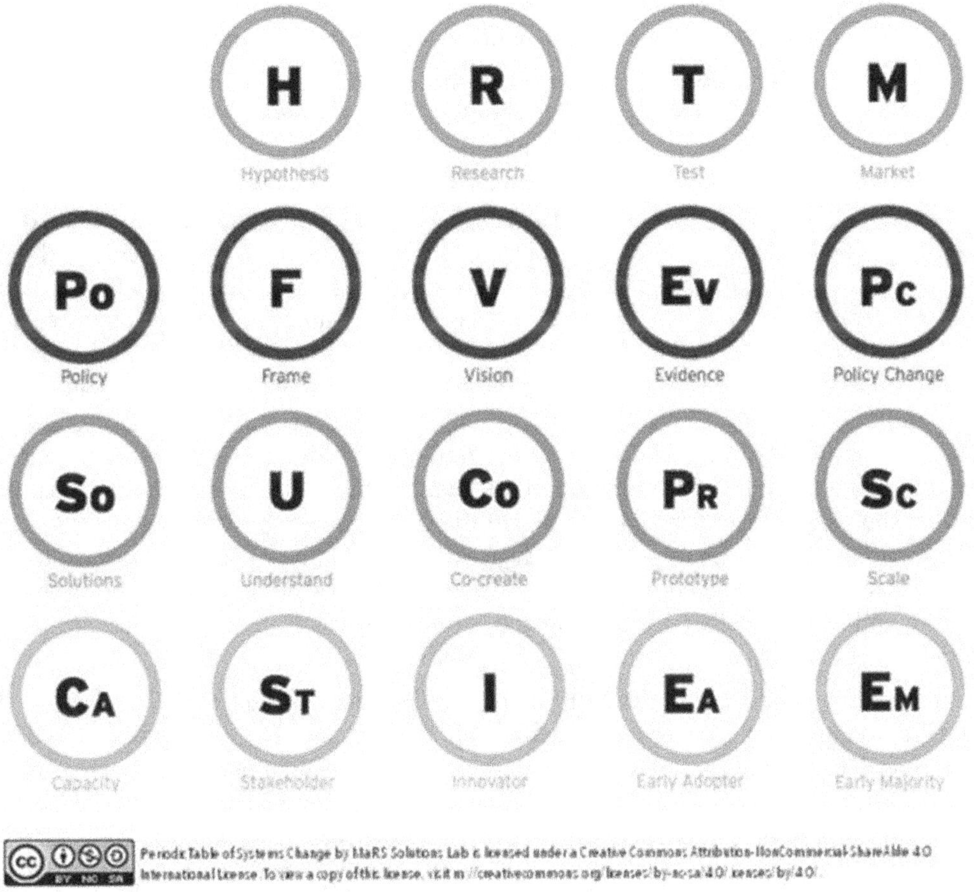

Source: MaRS Solution's Lab Approach (2017).

With an overall working methodology in place, MaRs developed an initial working plan for the project in July 2015. Desk research followed and public safety and insurance issues were identified as key in both the fields of transportation and accommodation. At the same time, research found that most citizens did not perceive a substantive difference between services (e.g. taxis versus Uber), as the majority of consumers did not prioritise the same issues as the regulatory regime, such as guaranteeing safety during service provision. The main question seemed to be how new technology approximated current provisions and practices used by the taxi industry. Taxi companies utilise background checks as a precondition for security and cameras on dashboards once a driver is on the road. Uber employs technological solutions to provide security using a digital trail to capture who was in the car, who was driving, where they went and for how long.

In order to understand the ramifications of this issue, the team set out to identify the main stakeholders in the system. They found that the final consumers of services were not as informative as the end users of regulation. In other words, it was not citizens but taxi drivers and hoteliers that provided insights into the system as a whole. The team interviewed sharing economy experts from both the public and private sectors, in order to better understand how the new system worked both for and against traditional businesses.

An early discovery was that AirBnB operates in a totally different market from that of traditional hoteliers, and that the nature and power of hotel-related unions differed substantially from the taxi industry in Toronto. Within the transportation sector, employment as a taxi driver was much more precarious than commonly understood, because garage and plate owners had consolidated more power than the actual drivers.

The taxi industry was already upset with the city because Uber had been active for two years prior to launching UberX, using their app to dispatch rides to existing taxi drivers – maintaining that they were just a technology company and not a taxi company – while building up a client base. After launching UberX, the company changed its operations and initiated what was perceived as an anti-taxi campaign with statements such as "the taxi industry is stuck in the 11th century". Thus, the city was seen by the taxi industry as the "cause of the pain" and "wilfully neglectful" by delaying action, thereby making stakeholders within a fragmented industry distrustful of government involvement. A neutral arbiter was needed to listen to all stakeholders' points of view and then render a picture of the situation that approximated the reality. As a new, non-governmental actor, MaRS Solutions Lab was seen as working with a degree of objectivity on a conflicted topic. As a more objective arbiter of the debate between the taxi industry, Uber and the city, the lab enjoyed "a different kind of relationship". In designing their research process, the MaRS team worked to balance different interests and to combine research with enabling activities that would keep discussions productive. The lab also tried to curb the violence that had erupted between taxi drivers and Uber drivers, and to bring the taxi industry and Uber together by treating the representatives not as organisations, but as individuals.

In order to understand the sharing economy problem better, MaRS Solutions Lab conducted ethnographic interviews with taxi drivers and Uber drivers, as well as stakeholders in the hospitality sector. Solutions Lab team members interviewed drivers from the back seat of taxis, at informal coffee stands and anywhere they conducted their work. This represented a significant procedural departure from a traditional research approach, as it bypassed usual channels (e.g. university ethics boards, etc.). Design research methodologies enabled the lab to get closer to the problem more quickly, without activating the machinery of the academic research community. The work also revealed the lived experience of participants in the sharing economy.

By leveraging desk research and ongoing interviews, MaRS Solutions Lab used process mapping to describe the existing regulatory "journeys" of stakeholders and thereby reverse engineered the regulatory system. This proved to be incredibly useful to public officials, both in the city and the province, who understood the system only in abstract terms that typically emphasised the importance of regulations. The work revealed the substantial burden placed on the taxi industry, the public value of which was not entirely clear. The way in which the debate was framed thus had to be redefined around core objectives for taxi drivers and the sharing economy.

To "elevate the general level of discussion" and spur stakeholders to speak the same (or at least a shared) language, a forum was organised in October 2015, three months after the launch of the project. Building capacity (like shared language) was understood to be crucial to overcoming siloed-thinking in different levels of government and among stakeholders. During the forum, lab team members used design methods to help participants outline value and actor-network maps for the sector. Interestingly, the maps drawn by government officials were quite consistent and illustrative of departmentalised thinking: civil servants understood the roles and responsibilities of their ministry or unit, but did not look far beyond the limits of their administrative authority. As such, the forum mostly highlighted gaps in knowledge, but also proved useful in helping MaRS identify all the stakeholders connected to the sharing economy and make necessary connections between civil servants and the private sector. Additionally, the forum provided an opportunity for the participants to engage in a debate with "intellectual honesty", rather than via combative platforms such as the news media. As some participants observed:

> *MaRS created a safe space for discussion. There was a lot of fear. But they created a kind of proxy for experimentation.*

> *If the government [had] run it, people would have come with the traditional mind-set; venting about the same things.*

Over the following months – November and December – the research team delved further into the perspectives and issues of stakeholders by continuing interviews, holding one-to-one meetings and exploring early suggestions for possible solutions. Encounters with policy makers, regulators, companies and associations helped both to inform the lab's understanding of the problem and to create buy-in and credibility for the three focused workshops that followed.

At the end of January, MaRS held the first one-day workshop on the sharing economy as a whole. The Solutions Lab invited participants with international experience on the sharing economy to share different models (e.g. Amsterdam) with the stakeholders. MaRS also used different mapping and creative exercises to help people envision possible futures and overall development goals for Toronto, especially with regard to the sharing economy. For example, the Hill Valley Telegraph exercise asks participants to imagine the front page of a newspaper in the future, to encourage them to think about innovation within the city.

The second workshop focused on transportation and was held at the beginning of February 2016. Three levels of government – city, province and federal – were present. MaRS Solutions Lab identified licensing, insurance, taxation and public safety as the main issues that regulation would likely need to address, and the workshop was designed in part to validate their research. Mapping exercises highlighted the findings of the desk research and interviews suggested that there was a heavy regulatory burden on taxi drivers, while the emerging car-sharing industry was struggling with an insurance product gap (a lack of liability insurance specific to the part-time working model of Uber drivers) – an issue that the province was working on in parallel.

Over the course of the seminar, the MaRS team presented carefully mapped regulatory journeys of taxi drivers (Figure 3.15) and used personal quotes from interviews of taxi *and* Uber drivers to illustrate their "lived experience". One of the most powerful quotes came from a taxi driver comparing his struggles with the city administration to those of Uber drivers: "I want them to feel my pain". This had the effect of joining together the realities of both sides of the debate. The lab also shared international experience on regulation (from Portland, Oregon and other cities) to highlight different potential futures for Toronto. A third, similar workshop on the topic of accommodation was held later in February, and used similar exercises and journey maps (Figure 3.16), but as the intensity of conflict was lower in the sector, the focus of attention remained squarely on transportation. Interestingly, nothing substantially new emerged from the workshops for the research team, but a common language around the problem began to develop among stakeholders. However, the regulatory journeys were surprising to many and provided new insights for many public officials, who had not previously considered the situation from this perspective.

Figure 3.15. Regulatory journeys of taxi drivers

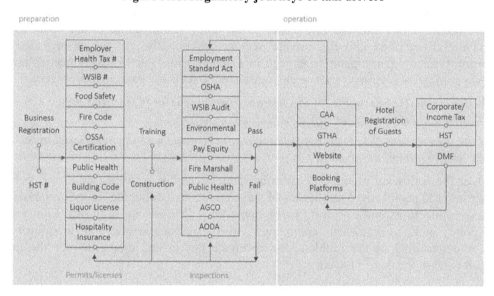

Source: Van den Steenhoven 2016a.

Figure 3.16. Regulatory journeys of hoteliers

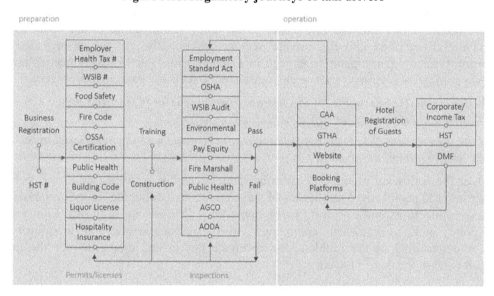

Source: Van den Steenhoven (2016b).

MaRS Solutions Lab thus helped to identify issues that would later help them develop simple solutions by using plain language, focusing on public value and utilising the appropriate level of regulation. The creation of a common language with which to talk about the problem was seen as the major benefit of the process: "MaRS took the concept to the next level". Furthermore, by facilitating an open, transparent process, MaRS was able to break down barriers between different silos, interests and organisations, which made the process much faster than usual.

In parallel with the workshops, MaRS continued conducting one-on-one interviews with experts and main stakeholders. This helped to build relationships and enabled the lab to validate approaches and answer questions such as: Will this work? Could it work in this way? It also helped to build capacity and increase a sense of ownership among the participants. The early months of 2016 were especially important for communication between the city of Toronto, the Municipal Licensing and Standards Division and the MaRS Solutions Lab, as the lab and the city needed to align their activities in order to influence the system effectively.

While the MaRS process was underway, the city initiated its own consultation process with stakeholders. As one official said, "with Uber, the devil is in the details". This process became the focal point for regulators, and for six months the Municipal Licensing and Standards Division transformed into a so-called "Uber bunker". Through compiling their own staff report on car-sharing and the taxi industry for the city council, the city officials came to recognise the value of the connections and discussions MaRS Solutions Lab facilitated: "On our own we are isolated, what gave us a leg up was going out from our [bubble]." Working together enabled the lab and the city to ensure that their reports and understanding of the issues were in alignment. In parallel, the city worked with the province to ensure a viable insurance option for Uber drivers existed by the time regulation was passed in the city of Toronto. Although the Ontario Ministry of Finance was able to design the framework for a new insurance model, private insurance companies would need to offer an insurance product that met the government's objectives. One problem was that the insurance companies did not understand where the risks resided in the ride-sharing business. Fortunately, the MaRS Solutions Lab workshops provided the province with an insight into the topic and contacts with key stakeholders, and they were able to develop a solution quickly. By February 2016, an insurance company was offering a dedicated product, enabling the city and province to move forward with regulation.

MaRS Solutions Lab released their final report on regulation and the sharing economy at the end of March 2016. Ten days later, the staff report of the City of Toronto was also released. The MaRS report was easily "digestible" and pragmatic offering practical, balanced recommendations, which set the stage for the City Council's regulatory decisions on the taxi industry and car-sharing. It succeeded by providing a balanced approach, while simultaneously creating a "correct political framework" that allowed a productive discussion about the key topics: legalising the sharing economy, meaningful solutions and a level playing field.

The timing of the MaRS report also played an important role. By releasing their report first, MaRS Solutions Lab absorbed much of the media attention, while opening the topic up for public discussion and giving the city space to make their recommendations. The report is widely perceived as representing the interests of citizens. However, neither Uber nor the taxi industry was totally satisfied (although neither directly opposed the report). Many issues are left open-ended – labour issues are not discussed at all – with the result that certain topics, such as the "level playing field", remain open to interpretation.

In April, the staff report went through committee, but was cut down and significantly changed by the City Council. Many politicians on the council had held their positions since 1998, when the owner-operated taxi model was voted into place, and as stewards of the existing model were resistant to change. Some city officials therefore defended the existing regulatory regime, and at points the process became very personal (officials claimed to have "Uber silver" in their hair by the end of the public debate). Some stakeholders found this political process to be unpredictable and, thus, disconcerting. It culminated, however, in July 2016 with a vote, and the City Council passed the new car-sharing and taxi regulation.

During this process the political support of the Mayor was essential. He took the issue up personally and returned parts of the regulation to the council floor, making it a key political issue of his mandate. While the Mayor has only one vote on the floor – there are no significant partisan coalitions in Toronto – he has political clout and ultimately helped ensure that the regulation was both substantive and passed. As one observer noted, "if the city [had not] adopted the regulation then the technology sector in the Toronto-Waterloo region would have looked stupid." This hints at a certain "innovation bias" on the part of the MaRS Solution Lab.[19]

In the end, the ride-sharing regulation passed by the council mandated that individuals working as Uber drivers in the City of Toronto must hold a Private Transportation Company (PTC) license obtainable from the city through the company. Drivers must also comply with the technical requirements for their vehicles (e.g. vehicles must be no older than seven model years) and hold and provide proof to the city of USD 2 million in liability insurance. Once a year, Uber drivers must submit to a background screening concerning their driving history and criminal record. Taxis also obtained the right to charge surge pricing, if rides are booked through a smartphone app.

Impact and effects

There are winners and losers in every process. Uber was likely the biggest winner in this case, as the process resulted in friendly regulation in Toronto, which will surely influence the rest of Canada.

Taxi medallion owners lost the most: the value of the medallion dropped from 300 000 dollars to 50 000 dollars, although it is hard to discern how much of that drop in value was due to the regulation. Some argued that the taxi drivers "bought from the city a full-time job with no cost to the city; taxi drivers paid for the privilege". Ultimately, there was little change for taxi drivers. However, the 17-day training programme was scrapped and meters are no longer inspected by the city. But the meter fee from the city and licensing remain, the latter necessitating more documentation than is needed for Uber drivers. For them, "a level playing field never really happened".

There are still many areas where a solution is pending – taxation and labour relations in particular are at the forefront of concerns. Taxi drivers are afraid they are at risk of losing revenue for their retirement. Also, the long-term socio-economic effects from factors such as the increase in precarious work are unclear. These issues are very complex and include impacts from economic development and growing inequality, which have yet to be evaluated. Other new challenges are also emerging, such as autonomous vehicles, which are leading regulators to ask whether the issue of Uber and taxi drivers will be redundant in a few years. Regulators are cautious of locking themselves into subpar solutions early on, but do not want to miss opportunities to influence the new industry.

Although the process facilitated by MaRS gave the taxi industry a chance to be heard, they seem to have lost trust in government as a result. Although Uber branded itself initially as a technology company, the same type of service providers in the taxi industry were regulated as taxi companies. As one member of the taxi industry said, "it left a bad taste in my mouth; we felt foolish that we followed the law." Nevertheless, the taxi lobby has quietened down and there have been no more protests or violence.

Many questions remain unanswered. There was hope that Uber would solve the "first mile, last mile problem" (i.e. the comfortable distance from a fixed-route transportation stop), however this remains to be seen. Does car-sharing really reduce congestion in the city? While many presume that it has an effect, the arrival of Uber has also introduced cars that otherwise would not have been on the roads. Additionally, less people are using public transportation while Uber cars commute from other areas to the city, which creates discussion around tolling highways. Another key question is whether the playing field can be characterised as fair if Uber drivers do not declare taxes. Indeed, taxes are an ongoing, complex issue at the federal level. There are still a lot of unknowns in this regard, and the government lacks access to the relevant Uber data (the company argues that it is protecting its business model). As one interviewee noted, "it takes a level of heroism to run with such an issue inside government."

AirBnB, meanwhile, is more controllable due to its platform, as has been demonstrated in many cities. Cities such as Washington DC in the United States are making progress on the taxation side and creating an example for the rest of the world to follow.

As time goes by, the relevance of the MaRS Solutions Lab report on the sharing economy lessens. However, its impacts are likely to be felt on a larger scale. As more municipalities legalise sharing economy businesses a critical mass will emerge, resulting in a domino effect. This trend is already underway: "Municipalities are phoning … Toronto and asking: What did you do?"

Did regulators really take a proactive stance by participating in the process with MaRS Solutions Lab? Maybe, but time will tell. The city is currently experiencing what is described as an "Uber hangover", with work on regulation in the accommodation sector proceeding at a slower pace. The province and the federal government are still struggling with the effects of silos. Thus, the majority of systemic impacts from the process are found outside government. However, more and more similar horizontal cross-cutting issues are entering the public domain in Canada, with examples including FinTech, automated vehicles and marijuana legislation. The need for organisations such as MaRS Solutions Lab in this context is clear.

The "black box" approach to policy making is changing and more consensus-based discussions are in demand – especially those that use third-party arbiters in public engagement processes by first defining what the problem is, then working through propositions in an open and transparent process. As one interviewee explained: "Problems cannot be too small, nor too big … for these kinds of processes. They have to be middle scope." If a long implementation process is foreseen, the question must be asked "will it be useful to know these people two years down the line and teach them the same vocabulary, so they can talk and understand each other?" Meanwhile, governments are struggling to find time for these multi-day processes, and a broad range of competing interests are demanding attention at the table.

Notes

1   This quotation and others used in the case studies are taken from interviews conducted for this report (see Annex 4). All quotations are anonymous in keeping with the research design.

2   *To Keep the Window Open*, presentation, Suðurnes Police.

3   Sigríður was Commissioner in a small police district until 2007, when she became the first female Deputy National Commissioner. On 1 January 2009 she was appointed Suðurnes Chief of Police and on 1 September 2014 she became the first female Chief of the Metropolitan Police.

4   See www.kokeilunpaikka.fi.

5   The government's assessment and research activity or "TEAS" (*Tutkimus, Ennakointi, Arviointi, Selvitys* or government analysis, assessment and research activities) was a consequence of the "Comprehensive Reform of State Research Institutes and Research Funding", a government resolution of September 2013.

6   See www.demoshelsinki.fi/en/demos-helsinki.

7   Some of the questions outlined in the proposal were: What are the best practices for the implementation of steering policies and operating experiments and policy pilots at the state-level internationally? What kind of management tools do these include and how are behavioural insights utilised in the approach and methods implemented? What would the strengthening of such an approach in Finland require in practice (e.g. what changes would be needed to legislation, steering and management, organisational structure, policies and operating culture)? What can be learned from the private sector and other countries' similar practices and models (cf. the Mindlab model or the "nudge" function used in the UK)?

8   Examples include: UK Cabinet Office (2011), "Open Public Services White Paper"; NESTA/UK Cabinet Office (2012), "Innovation in policy: Allowing for creativity, social complexity and uncertainty in public governance"; European Commission (2013), "Powering European public sector Reform: Towards a new architecture"; SITRA (2014), "Government for the future: Building the strategic and agile state"; and Valtiovarainministeriö (2014), "OHRA: Päätoksistä muutoksiin".

9   See Demos Helsinki (2015) for an English version of the report.

10   For more information, see: http://blogi.kansanelakelaitos.fi/arkisto/3648.

11   More about the organisational visioning process can be found in van Veelen et al. (2017).

12   For example, one participant stated: "In one case, we went to court and took the kids away from the same family three times in the last six months and nothing changed; the next day they were back with their family. I said that I won't do that anymore. Things needed to change."

13   This is a Vanguard term denoting a process in which a programme is scaled by repeating the same process internally within an organisation.

14   Indeed, the organisation has also been internationally acknowledged: CYPSA won the European Public Sector Award for the category of local government in 2015.

15   One CYPSA employee explained: "There are two types of waiting lists – new families are weighted on children's safety and if it is not critical then they are put on the waiting list. But can we be sure that they are safe 3 hours from the evaluation, the next day? The other type is when the case workers leave and cases are taken over by others."

16   The Mowat Centre is an independent public policy think tank in Ontario. The report can be found here:
      https://mowatcentre.ca/wp-content/uploads/publications/106_policymaking_for_the_sharing_economy.pdf.

17   See www.marsdd.com/about/story.

18   See www.marsdd.com/systems-change/mars-solutions-lab/mars-solutions-lab-overview.

19   While MaRS was generally seen as an objective/outside arbiter due to its connection to the MaRS Discovery District, some interviewed stakeholders were not surprising that the lab reached a sharing economy-friendly solution. The MaRS Solution Lab itself bases its credibility on three factors: its status as an innovation hub, the personal relationships it creates with stakeholders and simply *"hard work"*.

References

Alexander, J.F. and D. Kopp (2008), *Functional Family Parole and Probation Services.* FFT-LLC Inc, Seattle, WA.

Annala, M. (2016), *The Story of Demos Helsinki*, Experimentation and Demos Helsinki, Presentation, www.slideshare.net/secret/e9Ov4XKnvcn9i.

Berg, A., M. Hildén and K. Lahti (2014), *Kohti Kokeilunkultuuria* [Towards Experimental Culture]. SITRA (Finnish Fund for Research and Development), Helsinki, https://media.sitra.fi/2017/02/24015320/Selvityksia77.pdf.

Berg, A. (2013), Kokeilun paikka! Suomi matkalla kohti kokeiluyhteiskuntaa [Experiment place! Finland on the way to an experimental society]. *Eduskunnan Tulevaisuusvaliokunnan Julkaisu*, Vol. 1/2013, www.eduskunta.fi/FI/tietoaeduskunnasta/julkaisut/Documents/tuvj_1+2013.pdf.

CAEPV (Corporate Alliance to End Partner Violence) (n.d.), *Financial Costs.* CAEPV, Bloomington, IL, www.caepv.org/getinfo/facts_stats.php?factsec=2.

Council of Europe (2014), *Overview of Studies on the Costs of Violence Against Women and Domestic Violence.* Council of Europe, Strasbourg, France, https://rm.coe.int/CoERMPublicCommonSearchServices/DisplayDCTMContent?documentId=090000168059aa22.

Demos Helsinki (2016), *Näkökulmia Kokeilurahoitukseen: Ehdotus Kokeilurahoitusalust an Perustamisesta* [Perspectives on Pilot Support – Creating a Pilot Financing Platform], Selvitys- ja tutkimustoiminnan julkaisusarja, Vol. 14/2016, http://tietokayttoon.fi/documents/10616/2009122/14_N%C3%A4k%C3%B6kulmia+kokeilurahoitukseen.pdf/1162092d-a2cd-4424-95c0-b3051bc1ed1f?version=1.0.

Demos Helsinki (2015), *Design for Government: Human-centric Governance Through Experiments*, Government's Analysis, Assessment and Research Activities, www.demoshelsinki.fi/wp-content/uploads/2015/09/Design-for-Government-%E2%80%93-Governance-through-experiments.pdf.

Dinkgreve, M. (2016), Youth Protection Amsterdam. Purpose – Measures – Method: Every child safe – forever. Presentation.

DMCPI+ (2015), *Back to the Future: A Sharing Economy – A Report for DMCPI.* Privy Council Office, Government of Canada, Ottawa, www.pco-bcp.gc.ca/index.asp?lang=eng&page=innovation&doc=rpt1/index-eng.htm.

Experimental Finland (2016), Website, Prime Minister's Office, Helsinki, http://kokeilevasuomi.fi/en/frontpage.

Government of Ontario (2014), *Ontario Open for Business – Fewer Burdens, Greater Growth: Burden Reduction 2013 Highlights.* Ontario, Queen's Printer for Ontario, https://dr6j45jk9xcmk.cloudfront.net/documents/866/medte-burden-report-en.pdf.

Jónsson, S. and H.Ó. Einarsdóttir (2016), To keep the window open: Tackling domestic violence in Iceland. Visit from OECD regarding Domestic Violence, Sudurnes 29 November 2016.

Kalliomaa-Puha, L, A.K. Tuovinen and O. Kangas 2016. "The basic income experiment in Finland", *Journal of Social Security Law*, Vol. 23/2: 75-88.

Kangas, O. et al. (2017), "Final report for the Finnish basic income experiment recommends that the experiment be expanded", *Kelan Tutkimusblogi*, 11 January 2017, http://blogi.kansanelakelaitos.fi/arkisto/3648.

Kyvsgaard, B. and A. Snare (2007), "Vold mod kvinder. En- eller flerdimensionel?", in A. von Hofer and A. Nilsson (eds.), *Brott i välfärden. Om brottslighet, utsatthet och kriminalpolitik. Festskrift till Henrik Tham.* Kriminologiska institutionen. Stockholms universitet, Stockholm, pp. 181-202.

MaRS Solution's Lab (2017), *Our Approach.* MaRS Discovery District, Toronto, Canada, www.marsdd.com/systems-change/mars-solutions-lab/mars-solutions-lab-approach.

OHRA Project Group (2014), *From Decisions to Changes: Reforming the Government's Steering Framework – Report and Recommendations of the OHRA Project.* Report of the OHRA Project Group, http://valtioneuvosto.fi/documents/10184/1190126/OHRA-raportti-en.pdf/79db9e53-6929-475b-90fa-87fb7aae508f.

Prime Minister's Office (2016), *Experimental Finland – Making it happen?* Presentation, 2 December 2016.

Schön, D.A. (1987), *Educating the Reflective Practitioner: Toward a New Design for Teaching and Learning in the Professions.* Jossey-Bass, San Francisco, CA.

Sigurvinsdóttir, R. (2016), *Together Against Domestic Violence.* Presentation to the OECD, 28 November 2016.

Van den Steenhoven, J. (2016a), *Sharing Economy Transportation – Research Findings,* 5 February 2016. MaRS Solutions Lab, Toronto, Canada.

Van den Steenhoven, J. (2016b), *Sharing Economy Accommodations – Research Findings,* 10 February 2016. MaRS Solutions Lab, Toronto, Canada.

Van Veelen et al. (2017), "Embedding the notion of child- and family-centered care into organizational practice: Learning from organizational visioning", *Journal of Public Child Welfare.* Forthcoming.

Wauters, B. and M. Drinkgreve (2016), Improving the Quality of Public Service and Reducing Costs: Lessons from the Youth Protection Agency of Amsterdam (Netherlands). Case study. Mortsel, Belgium, www.latitudeconsulting.eu/images/childprotect.docx.

World Economic Forum (2010), *The Global Gender Gap Report.* WEF, New York.

Further reading

Dinkgreve, M. (2014), GGW – FFPS: Generiek Gezinsgericht Werken – Functional Family Parole Services.

Conclusions

This section is divided into two parts. The first provides an overview of the main conclusions drawn from the case studies and how they link to the analytical framework presented in the report. The second discusses the remaining challenges and opportunities arising from the introduction of systems approaches in the public sector. It also distils advice to policy makers concerning how and when to use system approaches, and the level of understanding required to drive successful system transformation processes.

Lessons from the case studies: Application of the systems transformation framework

While the way in which system transformation evolves depends on time and contextual factors, it is often triggered by "perception" of a crisis. This may take the form of an actual crisis or an understanding that current outcomes from systems are no longer acceptable. It also implies that someone needs to take direct ownership of the problem.

All the case studies examined in this report exhibit some level of urgency (e.g. a new business model entering the marketplace, drastically worsening situations, audits, evaluation reports, etc.), which galvanised the systems change process. This in turn created a window of opportunity, but did not guarantee success. Would the domestic violence project in Suðurnes have developed if Iceland had not experienced a social or fiscal crisis? Probably not. In short, the acknowledgement of cumulative severe effects can lead to a sense of urgency or crisis. However, the case study from the Netherlands indicates that it is difficult to start change processes during truly chaotic moments in organisations, as some level of stability has to be reached in order to apply a broader systems approach. Hence, the fiscal situation of the organisation was dealt with first, and then a more concerted effort towards systems change was put in motion. However, the stakeholders involved in such situations need to retain a sense of urgency, even in a stable environment. This is an essential part of changing systems in more static conditions. At the highest level, people need to acknowledge that public services and broader systems do not fulfil their intended purpose.

While understanding that there is a problem is the first step – even if it has not been clearly defined – it is not enough. This knowledge has to become actionable. The report identifies several tactics that act as important elements of systems change: people and place, dwelling, connecting, framing, designing, prototyping, stewarding and evaluating. However, every wicked problem is essentially unique, which precludes direct comparison between systems tactics in many cases. The case studies present a variety of conditions and contexts, political interests and involved actors. Consequently, different mixtures of systems tactics proved to be important, while all are present in some way in the case studies.

First and foremost, *people and place* **are essential drivers of a change process**. This not only pertains to leadership capabilities – although all the case studies display excellent characteristics in this regard – but also to the fact that there is a supporting team behind each change, a critical mass of people that believe that change is necessary and who have internalised the "crisis". Examples include the "Three Amigos" leadership structure in Iceland or the concerted effort of the director's board in the Netherlands. Having the "right people" around the table to discuss complex issues, outline processes and take ownership is key to the success of systems change. In terms of the *place* of change, it is interesting that all the case studies established an "objective place" to debate the need for change. In some form or another, an objective/independent arbiter was present for the discussion. Appointing such a body is crucial to the process. Otherwise, who among the stakeholders has the legitimacy to state whether or not the process is proceeding correctly? Government bodies, for their part, sometimes have long track records with outside stakeholders, which can undermine trust in a fair and unbiased process. Thus, in Canada a relatively new organisation (MaRS Solutions Lab) carried out the analysis and facilitated conversations, while in Finland an outside government party (Demos Helsinki) bore the brunt of the discussions. In Iceland, a steering committee for domestic violence was established in Reykjavik's Office of Human Rights to scale up the pilot phase (Suðurnes) to the metropolitan area. The office was not directly involved in the services and, thus, could provide a neutral ground for the discussions. In the Netherlands, the systems consultant acted the part, but a group within the organisation (not linked to the leadership) was created to become "tour guides" for the change process. These independent arbiters proved essential largely because each case was linked to a strong debate on values. Other organisations and networks have taken up this task beyond the cases discussed here. For example, in the United Kingdom, the independent What Works Network is creating, sharing and using high-quality evidence to influence policy makers and large professional communities to make better decisions.

Once they have internalised "crises", organisations need to create room for *dwelling* – investing the time to understand and articulate both the problem and the objectives. In the case of the Netherlands, this meant long internal discussions and the identification of a new mission: "Every Child Safe, Forever". The organisation understood that they needed to focus on children's safety and to start treating adults as parents first and individuals second. In the case of Iceland, broader community discussions with the police, social services, child protection, the church and so on were initiated. These reaffirmed the notion that domestic violence is a public health issue and not a private matter, thus prioritising the social effects of violence over privacy. In Canada, the value debate was designed to form part of the dwelling process and utilised different mapping exercises. It was clear that more flexible, affordable transportation system was preferred over other concerns. The Finnish case is the most complex in this regard: initial conversations took place mostly at the meta-level and revolved around methodology, in particular the disconnect in the policy-making system and the lack of direct feedback from implementation to policy design. This brought to light both the positive and negative sides of experimentation in practice.

It is important to involve all important parties at this stage and take them through the same learning journey. Otherwise, it becomes difficult to explain to *de facto* outsiders why a new approach is needed. This was evident in both the Dutch and the Icelandic cases. Attempts by the child protection organisation in Amsterdam to explain their approach after the fact to a broader network of connected service providers proved quite difficult. In the Icelandic case, a small community project was scaled up to the metropolitan area by transferring the key people involved. This created a lot of resistance within the larger organisation, which was being presented with a ready-made solution developed elsewhere.

***Time* is an essential resource in systems change because people need to live through and experience the change, rather than being told about it by a third party**. This approach makes systems change far from easy, as established structures are resistant to change. While the change process may come with individual sacrifices for those involved in the process, once the changes are institutionalised they become more difficult to reverse. This was certainly the case in Iceland and is also the hope in Finland for the experimental policy design programme.

Time and other resources are needed to re-examine the purpose of public sector systems and the problems connected to them. Usually, only high-level leaders within organisations have the ability to allocate these assets. Thus, *stewardship* **of systems change is needed from the outset**. All the case studies show that systems change requires resources from both outside and inside government, as the strategic planning and procurement systems in the public sector are not suitable for this kind of work. Thus, specific financing measures had to be found in both Canada and Finland. In the case of the Netherlands, a substantial part of the funds required had to be collected from outside the organisation. Standard tenders are ineffective here, as systems change is based on a defined mission and then iterative development towards the focus, rather than long-term visions and defined actions. While the domestic violence project in Iceland was initially carried out without additional resources, this meant that police had to prioritise some tasks over others and, thus, create time for change. High workloads and a heavy burden on the system meant that this approach is not sustainable over the long term. In other cases, initiating systems change required a direct investment on the part of the government.

The process of *dwelling* **instigates a debate about how to define public value within the system.** *Connecting* **to different parts of the system is therefore essential**. This is important not only in terms of *who* is involved in the process, but *how* it is facilitated – tools, methods and so on – in order to build a common understanding around complex problems. *Design* approaches are often used as an enabling mechanism for this work. MaRS Solutions Labs created personas for taxi drivers and Uber drivers and visualised regulatory journeys to make their experiences easily relatable to all stakeholders. The involvement of all parties in the process led to the emergence of a common language around the problem, which helped to structure the subsequent debate. The same can be seen in the Finnish case, where Demos Helsinki established links with a variety of stakeholders – known as the "godparents of experimentation"– in order to advance the concept of experimentation in Finland. This process created ownership of the issues being discussed. In the Suðurnes project in Iceland, the stakeholders all lived close together in a small community (although they were not yet working together towards a common goal), but *connecting* became essential when scaling up the project. The Dutch case, as argued above, highlighted to some degree the dangers of not connecting to the broader system from the outset.

To focus discussion on the change required, it is necessary to *frame* **the debate**. Problem frames link the desired outcome with a defined approach to building a solution. This is especially important when it comes to political debate, where the past experience and ideology of stakeholders may affect participants' understanding of complex problems and their causes. Thus, concentrating on the next steps is essential when framing the debate in a constructive manner. In Canada, the political process surrounding sharing economy regulation proved very difficult to control – even when all steps were taken to prepare the public discussion – and the intervention of a political leader was required to bring the discussion back round to the topic. In the Finnish basic income case study (Box 3.2) the political debate was somewhat unfocused – with different narratives on the nature of future work, welfare traps and social participation all brought into the debate – but also too narrowly focused on specific issues. This experience could affect the whole experimental policy design programme in the future. In the Dutch case study, the process was somewhat sheltered from outside interference, but the mission to keep children safe was concretely framed inside the organisation to retain a focus on the changes needed. In Iceland, the whole public debate had to be slowly remodelled to examine domestic violence in a different way. Framing such wicked problems is important, as many competing topics can eclipse the urgency of change. However, this process is very difficult to control and filled with uncertainty. Consequently, it is essential to establish connections between the right people at the outset, in order to start developing a common language for talking about the problem.

When there are many unknowns, additional information must be generated to make decisions more manageable. In situations of uncertainty, additional steps must be taken to test solutions. This is what is described in the report as *prototyping*. Closely linked with the *design* of systems change, it revolves around the feedback loop between having ideas and taking action. In the Finnish case, the process aimed to introduce new working methods to government; however, the underlying momentum sought to create an iterative government that would be more adaptive and resilient when faced with uncertainty and complex policy problems. Creating new knowledge from experimentation allows different processes to be designed. In a small community in Iceland this took the form of "learning by doing", as feedback loops between implementers and policy designers were short or even non-existent. However, in broader contexts, testing solutions in situations where outcomes are unclear should be specifically kept in mind, because feedback loops are usually longer. This raises an important question: How can those involved in the process know if the system and its change are producing the desired effect?

Meaningful measurement **is key to complex problems, as causality is usually established in hindsight and the effects of interventions are very difficult to assess**. In the Netherlands, a specific measure was used to *evaluate* child safety – "acute child safety", and in Iceland, a new risk framework was adopted. In Finland, however, the lack of concrete, numerical measures from the outset will likely change the direction of the experimental policy design programme. In the Canadian case study, the whole process was initiated to produce a legitimate evaluation of the impetus for change. Consequently, *evaluation* – as part of the systems tactics presented in the report – is not only needed to report back on the impact, but is also a communications tool used to legitimise the process of systems change and the use of systems approaches themselves. The evaluation carried out by the Institute for Gender, Equality and Difference at the University of Iceland, regarding the domestic violence project, helped to keep the process going. MaRS Solutions Lab's evaluation, alongside additional federal and non-governmental reports, paved the way for the city of Toronto to advance the sharing agenda.

In addition to the tactics outlined above, a number of other factors emerged. First, contextual factors are essential for systems change. Timing is everything and supporting elements must come together to create a "window of opportunity". Second, different resources are needed for systems change – time, finances, capabilities and legitimacy, which also means top-notch leadership and stability in terms of political support.

However, leadership alone is not sufficient. Based on the case studies, it is difficult to say which factors were the most influential, but it is clear that different elements have to be in place to make change possible. Moreover, systems change is a continuous process and it is essential to ensure feedback with regard to unintended consequences and unforeseen conditions during the implementation phase and beyond. As the case studies show, after one part of the system is reformed, other ineffective parts become more visible.

Challenges and opportunities in the public sector

The previous section outlines the many reasons why systems approaches can be an arduous, albeit rewarding process. This is even more so in the public sector where organisational learning is challenging due to input-output evaluation systems, path dependencies and the need to coordinate action between various governance levels. Traditionally, governments are designed for stability, reliability and predictability, and resistance to change is not surprising. Nevertheless, many systems in the public sector need to be transformed in order to respond to 21st-century challenges.

When should public policy makers use systems approaches?

Systems thinking is not a panacea for all ills. Neither is design. Systems approaches, in general, are very time and resource-intensive, especially when used to transform the functioning of a policy system in practice. Hence, policy makers should consider carefully before initiating these processes, if they are indeed willing to implement large-scale changes within policy systems. Otherwise, the exercise will be largely wasted.

However, the many wicked problems characterising policy spaces imply a mismatch between organisational structures and problem structures. Systems approaches can be highly useful in such cases, as well as in cases where traditional specialisation of tasks or sectors in the government apparatus no longer respond to challenges. Possible policy areas that could benefit from a systems approach involving transboundary policy challenges include: climate change, internal security, immigration and integration, policing, education, health care and so on.

Many imminent problems require a rapid response (e.g. the present refugee crisis), however, policy makers are also confronted with known problems whose effects are more removed or remote, as in the case of climate change. Consequently, public pressure for policy change can vary considerably. Invariably in crisis situations the window of opportunity is wider, presenting opportunities to change, start over and dramatically reconfigure public service delivery. In most other cases, however, change initiatives have to contend with resistance from established institutions and protocols. Under more static conditions, some level of backing from high-level leadership is needed to legitimise change processes and to muster the authority to work against both internal and external resistance to change. Consequently, the need to legitimise systems level reform can vary from situation to situation.

There are several questions public policy makers need to analyse before attempting systems transformation:

- How complex is the problem needing to be addressed?
- Is the level of uncertainty connected to the problem or the policy process high (e.g. does the outcome depend on numerous stakeholders whose positions are

contradictory and actions difficult to control or is scientific knowledge about the problem lacking)?

- Where does the legitimacy for policy reform come from?
- How much time is available to implement changes?
- Is there high-level backing to implement systems change?
- Does the potential systems level change cross different governance levels?
- Are the stakeholders open to change and cooperation with the process?

If policy makers are dealing with complex problems with high levels of uncertainty, and they have legitimacy and backing to implement a significant reform, then a systems approach is appropriate.

How much should public managers and civil servants know about systems approaches?

Usually, systems approaches in the public sector are led by experts. The existing processes are analysed and a new system is elaborated with the help of teams of specialists (e.g. systems thinkers, designers, etc.). However, this group does not usually participate in the implementation of systemic change, nor in the longer-term learning process within organisations. Hence, public sector managers and administrators have to be aware of the systems connected to their policy areas, in order to advance the learning process. There is a difference, however, between being systems aware and being a systems specialist. This report does not suggest that all public managers and civil servants should become systems thinking specialists; rather, it is important for different public policy experts and managers to be aware of these approaches.

In general, *public managers* working with complex problems should have a general understanding of the systems they work with. For reflexivity[1] in their policy field, such general knowledge is beneficial: it is important to be aware of complex processes – for example, links within the system and the possibility of unintended consequences – in order to be able to identify and work on them. Furthermore, having such knowledge helps managers work with relative precision, make decisions under high levels of uncertainty, and understand the limits of intervention and the importance of experimentation. Public managers are usually those best positioned to start changing organisational processes by building up open-ended approaches; thus, some knowledge of the potential and value of systems thinking is needed.

Policy experts within specific fields should have more precise knowledge of how their policy systems work, the stakeholders involved and the possible causal relationships within the system. Even if such knowledge can never be precise, it is necessary so as to be able to understand the problems practitioners are working with and to build up open-ended practices to gain useful feedback. During efforts to promote systems change, policy experts work on the details, and put together teams to analyse processes and procure help from outside the public sector. As such, knowledge about the usefulness and limits of different systems approaches can be highly necessary. Do policy experts need help in simulating effects amid an over-abundance of data or require a more profound, objective perspective to outline the interdependencies within a policy system? Systems approaches and tools can differ considerably under these circumstances.

---

[1] This term refers to continuous learning from practise – reflection-in-action (see Schön, 1987).

Street-level bureaucrats play an important role in systems change, as they are closest to the end users, their needs and the effects. Consequently, they have first-hand knowledge of how a specific arm of the system is functioning, although they might not possess a full picture of the system. They should be included in the open-ended processes that systems approaches require, because they are usually the first to spot unintended consequences and can pass the feedback on to policy makers. However, to do so, they need to be aware of the overall goals of the systems. Hence, they have to be systems aware, especially in terms of the functions the systems are fulfilling.

The above does not imply that other groups of practitioners should not be involved in a more profound systems reform. Creating awareness of systems failures and shortcomings is necessary at all levels, from a public manager to a street-level bureaucrat, in order to create fertile ground for change.

How should public managers use systems approaches in the public sector?

As outlined above, there are various systems approaches which have more or less rigid methodologies. This report does not promote a single, specific systems approach – the selection of the method and the specific tools used depends on contextual elements and the policy problem in question. This point cannot be emphasised enough: the systems and design tools used will have their greatest effect when they are selected specifically to address the context, the problem, the timeline and the capacity of the organisations involved.

So how does a public manager know when a systems approach might be appropriate? The first indicator will be that their current tools and the logic that underpins the design of those tools no longer meet expectations, or are making the problem worse. The exhaustion of traditional problem-solving approaches also suggests that systems dynamics have changed the underlying architecture of the problem itself. In such cases, new analytical tools and problem solving methods will be needed. Another indicator might be that the problem in question cannot be solved under the sole authority of the administrative body or even within government itself. A second-order indicator could be demand from citizens to have a voice and role in the work of the administration, where none previously existed (or was treated as tangential). Finally, any problem that cannot be addressed via a large or small-scale single initiative, either because of cost and time constraints, difficulty in building sufficient constituencies or because of the complexity of the problem itself, will benefit from systems and design methodologies.

Once a systems problem has been identified, a course of action needs to be chosen. Two immediate courses can be taken. The first is to reflect upon who can help those involved understand the systems problem and how they might do this. This will likely require external expertise, but there will also undoubtedly be internal allies who have had similar experiences, and can give advice with regard to resourcing, procurement, buy-in and other issues specific to the context. In terms of external expertise, it is recommended to consult with designers and others with public sector experience, as the motives that drive decision making are very different in a public service context than, say, in product design. A good place to start is think tanks and universities working on innovation, complexity and operational research in virtually any context. For example, the Open University in the United Kingdom has extensive experience with systems thinking.

The second course of action is for managers to organise training opportunities both for themselves and their staff. These do not have to take the shape of a large, formal professional development scheme. They can start small; however the objective is to begin to discuss ideas on systems and complexity, and to foreground new ways of working with new type of problems. This could include inviting a speaker to come in and share insights into wicked problems and how they can be tackled. This will set a foundation for further exploration through formal training sessions that will help enable everyone to feel a measure of ownership and, most importantly, play a role in a changing administration.

Again, greater specificity will be highly dependent on the context, institutional capacity, problem, timeframe and resources available to public administrations, as they embark on systems change. However, this report highlights strategic principles in systems approaches that are essential to systems transformation success.

Annex 1.

Definitions

Ashby Space: the relationship between a variety of stimuli and a variety of responses (or in organisational terms, external complexity and internal complexity. When stimuli and response are in balance, this is called *requisite variety* (Boisot and McKelvey, 2011).

Complex adaptive system: a system often involving human activities and dynamics that make it continuously emergent and with only limited predictability.

Complexity gap: mismatch between the increased complexity and uncertainty of the world and the established governance arrangements and institutions of society.

Intervention: small-scale discrete or coordinated actions that can transform larger systems.

Linear causation: an understanding of each cause as the effect of a previous cause.

Soft systems methodology: a methodology used to support and structure thinking about, and intervention in, complex organisational problems.[1]

Stewardship: the art of aligning decisions with impact when many minds are involved in making a plan and many people participate in its enactment (Boyer, Cook and Steinberg, 2013).

System: elements joined together by dynamics that produce an effect, create a whole or influence other elements and systems. Systems exist on a spectrum of comprehensibility – from those easily observed and analysed to those that are highly complex or novel requiring postulation. A system always exceeds the sum of its parts.

VUCA: an acronym for Volatility, Uncertainty, Complexity and Ambiguity that describes the general state of global affairs today. The term was coined by the US Army War College to describe the fallout left by the end of the Cold War.

Window of opportunity: when separate streams of problems, policies and politics come together at certain critical times, then solutions become linked to problems, and both are tied to favourable political forces (Kingdon, 1995).

Window of viability: a balance between diversity and efficiency. Too much efficiency can lead to brittleness, whereas too much diversity can lead to stagnation.

Wicked problems: complex challenges where conflicting interests and priorities, and incomplete and contradictory information, make establishing shared facts and understanding difficult.

---

[1] See www.learnaboutor.co.uk/strategicProblems/m_s_3frs.htm.

References

Boisot, M. and B. McKelvey (2011), "Connectivity, extremes, and adaptation: A power-law perspective of organizational effectiveness", *Journal of Management Inquiry*, Vol. 20, No. 2, pp. 119-133.

Boulding, K.E. (1956), "General systems theory: The skeleton of science", *Management Science*, Vol. 2/3, pp. 197-208.

Boyer, B., J. Cook and M. Steinberg (2013), *Legible Practises: Six Stories About the Craft of Stewardship*. SITRA, http://helsinkidesignlab.org/legiblepractises.

Annex 2.

A brief history of systems approaches

Complex problems are not new and efforts to simplify them in order to make them "manageable" have long been on the agenda of policy makers and academics, and especially systems thinkers. While there are several streams of systems thinking (general systems theory, cybernetics, systems dynamics, etc.), there are thousands of different streams of "systems thought" with hundreds of different methods and techniques. Today, many policy studies have moved to apply methodological pluralism (choosing the method(s) based on the problem at hand) (Payne, 2006) when using systems approaches. However, it is important to understand the background of these different approaches before applying or insourcing analyses. No method is perfect and systems thinking and other similar methodologies should be understood as one of many tools available to governments.

Systems approaches have been around for more than 80 years (e.g. see Jackson, 2009). They are rooted in the works of von Bertalanffy and his General Systems Theory[1] and Boulding's (1956) contribution on hierarchical complexity. These strands largely originated from biological and ecological studies. During the Second World War, engineering studies advanced systems research, with operations research leading to the emergence of cybernetics and control theory (e.g. Ashby, 1956; Bateson, 1972; Wiener, 1948: 112; see also Beer, 1979) and systems engineering (Hall, 1962).

Cybernetics is a study that concerns itself with the flow of information through a system and the ways in which this information is used by the system to control itself (Mingers and White, 2010). One of the cornerstones of organisational cybernetics is the Ashby theorem on requisite variety (complexity).[2] The theorem states that simplifying complex problems does not bring us closer to workable solutions – complex problems usually also require complex action. Thus, public managers must have access to a variety of actions similar to the variety of circumstances they wish to control.

Cybernetics introduced several new themes to the debate, for example, the relationship between the peripherality (autonomy) versus the centrality (control) of actors within organisations, and the importance of variety and participative management. Cybernetics looks at the places where new ideas can grow within an organisation and the kind of autonomy necessary. Consequently, it is most useful as a *diagnostic and design tool for the development and viability of organisations* (Schwaninger, 2004: 414).

The surge in computing power after the Second World War made it possible to model larger systems with quantitative computer models leading to the formal study of *system dynamics* (Forrester, 1961, 1968). This created momentum to utilise mainly quantitative modelling to describe complex interactions and feedback in systems.

The early system dynamics proponents believed that certain generic feedback structures could be described and modelled (Forrester and Forrester, 1969). This also carried over into Peter Senge's work on learning organisations – *The Fifth Discipline* (Senge, 1990) – and system archetypes that are proposed to explain many organisational problems. This work is also echoed by Donella Meadows (2008: 3) including her "leverage points" and the twelve places to intervene in a system – see Figures A2.1 and A2.2. These approaches simplify the analytical process to a degree, making it easier to use, but also come at a cost: they concentrate on the theoretical expectations of problems – archetypical situations – but may miss the true causes of problems. Nevertheless, this simplification allows systems dynamics to identify various causal loops within the system and test the former in computer models and simulations. This can be a justifiable approach when substantial amounts of data need to be analysed (see the example in Box A2.1).

Figure A2.1. Meadows' leverage points

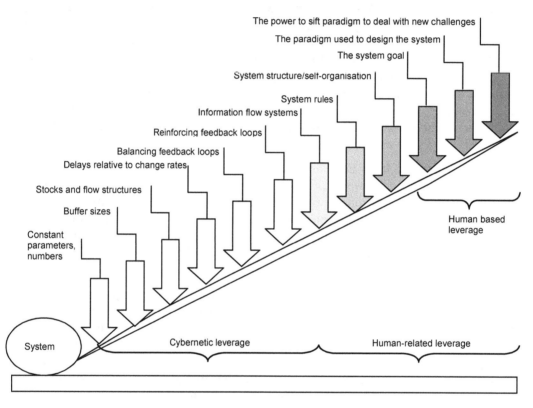

Source: Based on Meadows (1999).

Figure A2.2. Les Robinson's Adaptation of Meadows' leverage points

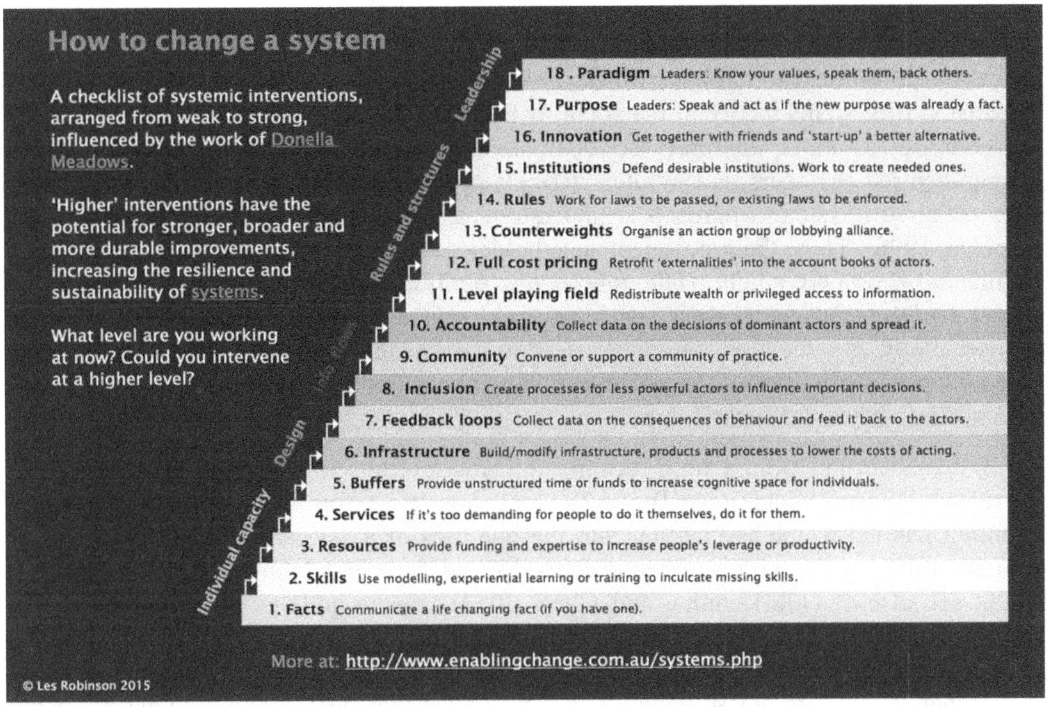

Source: Robinson (2015).

Box A2.1. Using simulations for obesity, National Collaborative on Childhood Obesity Research (USA)

Childhood obesity is a very complex problem that includes traditional risk factors (nutrition, physical activity, predisposition) and also environmental factors (interpersonal, community and intersectoral dynamics).

In 2009, the Centers for Disease Control and Prevention, National Institutes of Health (NIH), the Robert Wood Johnson Foundation and the US Department of Agriculture formed the National Collaborative on Childhood Obesity Research (NCCOR). The goal of the organisation was to address the growing childhood obesity epidemic in the United States by building research and surveillance capacity, and using innovation to stimulate systemic thinking in order to generate fresh, synergistic ideas to tackle the problem. The collaborative effort was also intended to help accelerate policy change based on system-based insights. In 2011, NCCOR launched the Catalogue of Surveillance Systems and the Measures Registry (www.nccor.org/measures) to make freely available resources on system characteristics connected to childhood obesity.

Two NCCOR affiliated networks, the Childhood Obesity Modeling Network and Envision, have implemented systems-based approaches focusing primarily on understanding childhood obesity in developed nations. For example, Envision tries to use computational simulation models to create learning laboratories that mimic reality and test virtually different combinations and sequences of childhood obesity interventions.

Sources: Bures et al. (2014); McKinnon et al. (2012).

Quantitative models of systems interactions generally rely on predefined goals and causal relationships (Jackson, 2009: S26). They therefore have limited applicability, especially concerning social systems, as they cannot be easily well applied to unstructured problems. Consequently, debate over systems dynamics in the social sciences has moved from modelling "external reality" to modelling people's subjective perceptions (see Lane, 2000). Since the late 1970s, *soft systems* approaches have emerged (Jackson, 2009) next to hard systems/system dynamics approaches, as a response to the expansion of systems theory to the social world (Checkland, 1999: 45-56). Soft systems methodology is more interpretivist, qualitative in nature and considered to be more human-centred (Mingers and White, 2010; Pepper, Sense and Speare, 2016: 135). In effect, the soft systems approach is understood as a continual process (Checkland and Scholes, 1990). Thus, the focus is on stakeholders, their views and learning as a process. While *hard systems engineering approaches analyse the system backwards from the desired objective, soft systems methodology begin by asking what the objective is.* Consequently, it is mostly useful when used to gain insight into the decision-making and planning process in systems. Nevertheless, there are critiques regarding the relative nature and subjectivity of the methodology.

While there has been a push recently towards multidisciplinary and methodological pluralism in many fields (see Box A2.2), the legacy of formal modelling in systems thinking has led to the assumption that the qualities of a "systems thinker" or rules of systems thinking can be discretely described (Anderson and Johnson, 1997; Meadows, 2008; see also Buckle Henning and Chen, 2012).[3] Some authors have concluded that without intensive training in systems methodologies success will be unlikely (e.g. Ledington and Donaldson, 1997). Thus, systems approaches have remained rather rigid when it comes to practice and it is not surprising that systems thinking has not come to the fore in many domains, especially public policy and management communities. However, this report specifically aligns itself with recent developments towards methodological pluralism and problem-based approaches to systems thinking and design. Hence, it calls on policy practitioners to avoid the paradigm trap of rigid utilisation and encourages them to synthesise different approaches.

Box A2.2. Towards methodological pluralism

Soft systems and system thinking, in general, has expanded in the social realm since the late 1980s and 1990s, when the latter was combined with complexity theory, network organisation and learning organisation theories (e.g. Kaufmann, 1995; Senge. 1990). The origins of complexity/chaos theory lie in chemistry, chaos and mathematics. This presents a challenge to the stability-based orthodoxy because it highlights the importance of instability, discontinuity and non-linearity. Consequently, soft systems methodology is now used to tackle wicked problems, while it is also understood that complex problems involve various phases and, therefore, different methodologies and approaches may be employed to achieve success (Mingers and White, 2010). This has led to the parallel development of critical systems theory (Ulrich, 1983), which sheds light on power relations in systems – usually an ignored dynamic in hard and soft systems theories and multi-methodology or methodological pluralism.

As systems approaches cover various tools and methodologies, both from the quantitative to the qualitative (from stock and flow/causal loop diagrams, participatory system mapping, group model building, cognitive mapping, mediated modelling and even SWOT analyses to strategic choice approaches, etc.), there is a lot to choose from.

Box A2.2. Towards methodological pluralism *(continued)*

Nevertheless, hard systems approaches have been more delineated and causal loop diagrams (CLDs) – based on systems dynamics/cybernetics – are still the most frequently utilised to visualise systems.[4] However, such approaches are not problem free. They describe causal relationships between selected variable sets focusing on both negative and positive feedback loops within a given system. Thus, CLDs usually describe existing patterns of systems and fail to describe future behavioural patterns of the system or provide deep insights into how to intervene in the system (Nemecskeri et al., 2008).

Recently, these methods have been extended to include participatory modelling approaches, for example participatory systems mapping, group model building and mediated modelling (Sedlacko et al., 2014). Participatory systems methods have also been increasingly applied in the field of natural resources (van den Belt et al., 2010). Furthermore, in practice, most systems approaches use a multitude of methods and no longer distinguish between the origins of ideas in detail.

Notes

1   See the historical overview in von Bertalanffy (1972).

2   "Only variety can destroy variety" (Ashby, 1956). This means that actors have to balance their own complexity/variety with the contextual/situational complexity/variety. This can be achieved by simplifying external variety or amplifying actors' own variety or both at the same time.

3   Buckle Henning and Chen highlight systems thinking orientations in six different categories: orientations towards causality, logic, particular data sources, explicit and implicit structures, subjectivity and self-reflection.

4   For example, in the field of sustainable consumption – see Jackson (2009) and Nemecskeri et al. (2008).

References

Anderson, V. and L. Johnson (1997), *Systems Thinking Basics.* Pegasus Communications, Cambridge, MA.

Ashby, W.R. (1956), An Introduction to Cybernetics. Chapman and Hall, London.

Bateson, G. (1972), "The logical categories of learning and communication", *Steps to an Ecology of Mind*, University of Chicago Press, Chicago, IL, pp. 279-308.

Beer, S. (1979), *The Heart of Enterprise (Vol. 2).* Wiley & Sons, New York.

Buckle Henning, P. and W.C. Chen (2012), "Systems thinking: Common ground or untapped territory?", *Systems Research and Behavioral Science*, Vol. 29/5, pp. 470-483.

Bumiller, E. (2010), "We have met the enemy and he is PowerPoint), *New York Times*, 26 April 2010, www.nytimes.com/2010/04/27/world/27powerpoint.html.

Bures, R.M. et al. (2014), "Systems science: A tool for understanding obesity", *American Journal of Public Health*, Vol. 104, p. 1156.

Checkland, P. (1999), *Systems Thinking: Rethinking Management Information Systems.* Oxford University Press, Oxford, UK.

Checkland, P. and J. Scholes(1990), *Soft Systems Methodology in Action.* Wiley, Chichester, UK.

Forrester, Jay W. (1968), *Principles of Systems* (2nd edn). Productivity Press, Portland, OR.

Forrester, Jay W. (1961), *Industrial Dynamics.* Productivity Press, Portland, OR.

Forrester, J.W. and J.W. Forrester (1969), *Urban Dynamics* (Vol. 114). MIT Press, Cambridge.

Hall, A.D. (1962), *A Methodology for Systems Engineering*, Van Nostrand Reinhold, New York.

Jackson, M.C. (2009), "Fifty years of systems thinking for management", *Journal of the Operational Research Society*, Vol. 60/1, pp. S24-S32.

Kaufmann, S. (1995), At Home in the Universe: the Search for the Laws of Complexity, Penguin, London.

Lane, D. (2000), "Should system dynamics be described as a 'hard' or 'deterministic' systems approach?", *Systems Research and Behavioural Science*, Vol. 17, pp. 3-22.

Ledington, P and J. Donaldson (1997), "Soft OR and management practice: A study of the adoption and use of soft systems methodology", *Journal of the Operations Research Society*, Vol. 48/3, pp. 229–240.

McKinnon, R.A. et al. (2012), "The National Collaborative on Childhood Obesity Research Catalogue of Surveillance Systems and Measures Registry", *American Journal of Preventive Medicine*, Vol. 42/4, pp. 433-435.

Meadows, D.H. (2008), *Thinking in Systems: A Primer*. Chelsea Green Publishing, White River Junction, VT.

Meadows D.H. (1999), *Thinking in Systems*. Sustainability Institute, Norwich, VT.

Mingers, J. and L. White (2010), "A review of the recent contribution of systems thinking to operational research and management science", *European Journal of Operational Research*, Vol. 207/3, pp. 1147-1161.

Nemecskeri, R. et al. (2008), *System Dynamics to Diagnose and Devise Patterns for Sustainable Consumption and Production*. Lund University Publications, Lund, Sweden.

Payne, G. (2006), Methodological pluralism", in *The SAGE Dictionary of Social Research Methods*, pp. 174-176, https://johnpostill.com/2012/10/31/methodological-pluralism.

Pepper, M., A. Sense and K. Speare (2016), "Systems pluralism in infrastructure decision-making for socially connected greenfield communities", *Systemic Practice and Action Research*, Vol. 29/2, pp. 129-148.

Robinson, L. (2015), "How to change a system (18 ways)", *Changeology*, 19 August 2015, https://changeologyblog.wordpress.com/2015/08/19/how-to-change-a-system..

Schwaninger, M. (2004), "Methodologies in conflict: achieving synergies between system dynamics and organizational cybernetics", *Systems Research and Behavioral Science*", Vol. 21/4, pp. 411-431.

Sedlacko, M. et al. (2014), "Participatory systems mapping for sustainable consumption: Discussion of a method promoting systemic insights", *Ecological Economics*, Vol. 106, pp. 33-43.

Senge, P. (1990), The Fifth Discipline: the Art and Practice of the Learning Organization. Currency Doubleday, New York.

Ulrich, W. (1983), *Critical Heuristics of Social Planning: A New Approach to Practical Philosophy*. Chichester, UK, Wiley.

van den Belt, M. et al. (2010), "Public sector administration of ecological economics systems using mediated modelling", *Annals of the New York Academy of Sciences*, Vol. 1185/1, pp. 196-210.

Von Bertalanffy, L. (1972), "The history and status of general systems theory", *Academy of Management Journal,* Vol. 15/4, pp. 407-426.

Wiener, N. (1948), *Cybernetics*. Hermann, Paris.

Further reading

Ackoff, R. (2006), Why Few Organizations Adopt Systems Thinking: Systems Research and Behavioural Science. John Wiley, New York.

Alter, M.J. (2004), *Science of Flexibility*. Human Kinetics, Champaign, IL.

Argyris, C. and D.A. Schon (1974), *Theory in Practice: Increasing Professional Effectiveness.* Jossey-Bass, San Francisco, CA.

Dawidowicz, P. (2012), "The person on the street's understanding of systems thinking", *Systems Research and Behavioral Science*, Vol. 29/1, pp. 2-13.

Eden, C. (1995), "Strategic options development and analysis (SODA)", in *Rational Analysis Revisited.* Operational Research Society, Birmingham.

Hamal, G. and C.K. Prahalad (1999), "Strategic intent", *Harvard Business Review*, (May-June), pp. 63-76.

Kelly, G.A. (1955), The Psychology of Personal Constructs. Volume One: A Theory of Personality. W.W. Norton, New York.

Kotiadis, K. and J. Mingers (2006), "Combining PSMs with Hard OR methods: the philosophical and practical challenges", *Journal of the Operational Research Society*, Vol. 57/7, pp. 856-867.

Lewin, K. (1947), "Frontiers in group dynamics II. Channels of group life; social planning and action research", *Human Relations*, Vol. 1/2, pp. 143-153.

Middleton, P. (ed.) (2010), Delivering Public Services That Work (Vol. 1): Systems Thinking in the Public Sector – Case Studies. Triarchy Press, Axminster, UK.

Midgley, G. (2000), "Systemic intervention", in *Systemic Intervention: Philosophy, Methodology, and Practice.* Kluwer/Plenum, New York, pp. 113-133.

Mulgan, G. and C. Leadbeater (2013), *Systems Innovation.* Nesta, London.

Reynolds, M. and S. Holwell (2010), "Introducing systems approaches", in M. Reynolds and S. Holwell (eds.), *Systems Approaches to Managing Change: A Practical Guide.* Springer, London, pp. 1–23.

Roy, J. and J. Langford (2008), Integrating Service Delivery Across Levels of Government: Case Studies of Canada and Other Countries. IBM Center for the Business of Government, Washington, DC.

Seddon, J. and C. Brand (2008), Debate: Systems Thinking and Public Sector Performance.

Von Hippel, E. (1994), "'Sticky information' and the locus of problem solving: Implications for innovation", *Management Science*, Vol. 40/4, pp. 429-439.

Weber, M. (1947), *The Theory of Social and Economic Organization.* Translated and edited by A.M. Henderson and T. Parsons. Oxford University Press, New York.

Zokaei, Z. et al. (2010), *Lean and Systems Thinking in the Public Sector in Wales.* Lean Enterprise Research Centre report for the Wales Audit Office. Cardiff University, Cardiff.

Annex 3.

Case study methodology

Systems approaches are rarely labelled as such. They tend to emerge out of a convergence of dynamics, such as inspired leadership, intractable challenges, access to competent stakeholders/partners and sometimes an unusual funding situation. The framework of systems transformation outlined in Chapter 2 has been used as a general approach to both case selection (identify cases where these processes are evident) and case analysis (understanding how these principles were applied in practice). The case study process in this report focused on understanding how a problem was framed or reframed so that a new solution and possibly methodology could emerge, and on the tactics or actions that were designed and executed with an eye toward systemic impact.

The case studies aimed at:

- Identifying areas in which systems thinking will be useful within the public sector.

- Providing insights into how systems approaches have been used in different public sector contexts including: differences in methodologies, legitimisation and approaches to uncertainty, etc.

- Outlining the contextual differences found in applying systems thinking in real-life situations.

- Identifying the challenges and possibilities for systems thinking within the public sector.

- Generating awareness about the potential of systems thinking in the public sector.

As systems approaches produce different kinds of impacts on governments and governance processes, the report has attempted to reproduce this variety through the selection of case studies. For instance, some systems approaches and subsequent innovations result in governments forming long-term working relationships with external partners, while others aim to embed a set of methodologies or even project teams into government itself and establish permanent capacity. It will be useful for public sector managers interested in systems approaches to discover the variety of responses possible given the variety of challenges and opportunities they face.

The case studies were selected based on prior desk research on the topic. The following criteria were applied to the selection process:

- The case study must deal with a public policy problem, although connected public service delivery can lie outside the public sector.

- The public policy problem must be complex and systematic in nature, with multiple interconnected explanations, no optimum solution, multiple stakeholders and high levels of uncertainty, etc.

- There must be a potential for transformative effects at the systems level (i.e. current solutions are failing or have limited impact).

- Systems approaches must have been used to analyse the problem.

- Cases will be selected from different policy areas (e.g. active and healthy aging, resource-efficient production and eco-innovation, transportation and public safety).

The case study analysis utilised desk research and, to the extent possible, interviews with stakeholders (and, if necessary, questionnaires). Through triangulation of data, the analysis explored:

- Why and which systems approaches were chosen to solve the policy problem.

- How systems analysis was carried out (what did the process entail, who were the stakeholders, which resources were used, how much time did it take).

- Whether the results of the analysis were implemented in public service delivery.

- What (endogenous and exogenous) challenges were encountered at different stages of the process.

- What were the perceived or measured effects of applying the approach.

The interviews were semi-structured and based on an interview guide utilising both inductive and deductive questions. Interviews were not recorded, but the information given was noted down. Findings and quotes from the former were anonymised to ensure openness among participants.

Annex 4.

Interviews conducted for this study

The following people were interviewed for the case studies:

- Joeri van den Steenhoven, Director of MaRS Solutions Lab, 11 October 2016 (teleconference).

- Mikko Annala, Demos Helsinki, 14 October 2016 (Skype).

- Alda Hrönn Jóhannsdóttir, Chief Attorney, and Marta Kristín Hreiðarsdóttir, Specialist, Metropolitan Police, Reykjavík, 28 October 2016 (Skype).

- Marc Dinkgreve, Ambassador of Knowledge, Jeugdbescherming Regio Amsterdam, 4 November 2016 (Skype).

- Anne Bermonte, Government of Ontario – MEDEI, Director, Open for Business Branch and Joeri van den Steenhoven, Director, MaRS Solutions Lab, 14 November 2016

- Joeri van den Steenhoven, Director, Idil Burale, Associate, and Claire Buré, Programme Manager, MaRS Solutions Lab, 14 November 2016.

- Ted Graham, PwC Canada Innovation Lead, 14 November 2016.

- Chris Schafer, Uber, Policy Manager, 14 November 2016.

- Peter Wallace, City Manager, City of Toronto, 15 November 2016.

- Tracey Cook, Executive Director and Vanessa Fletcher, Policy and Planning Advisor, Municipal Licensing and Standards, Carleton Grant, Director, Policy and Strategic Support, City of Toronto, 15 November 2016.

- Caroline Pinto, Managing Principal, Counsel Public Affairs Inc., 15 November 2016.

- Roberto Pegoraro, Senior Advisor and Technical Expert, Automobile Insurance Policy, Ministry of Finance – Financial Services Commission of Ontario, 15 November 2016.

- Daniel Skilliter, Senior Policy Advisor, Policy and Research, Office of the Premier, 15 November 2016.

- Frank Denton, Assistant Deputy Minister – Policy, Planning, and Oversight Division, Government and Consumer Services, 15 November 2016 (teleconference).

- Paul Devnich, Director (Acting) Programme Policy and Analytics Branch, Ontario Ministry of Revenue, 15 November 2016.

- Joeri van den Steenhoven, Director, Idil Burale, Associate, and Claire Buré, Programme Manager, MaRS Solutions Lab, 15 November 2016.

- Rodney Ghali, Assistant Secretary; Chad Hartnell, Director of Operations and David Donovan, Lead, Strategic Policy and Innovative Finance, Innovation Hub, Privy Council Office, Government of Canada, 16 November 2016.

- Anatole Papadopoulos, Executive Director, Policy Innovation for Canadian Heritage, Government of Canada, 16 November 2016.

- Kristine Hubbard, Operations Manager, Beck Taxi, 23 November 2016 (teleconference).

- Ericka Stephens-Rennie, Senior Analyst and Program Integration Coordinator, Environment Canada (prior Co-Lead on the Sharing Economy Project, Deputy Ministers' Committee on Policy Innovation, Government of Canada), 25 November 2016 (teleconference).

- Rannveig Sigurvinsdóttir, Postdoctoral Research Fellow, Reykjavík University, 28 November 2016.

- Alda Hrönn Jóhannsdóttir, Chief Attorney, and Marta Kristín Hreiðarsdóttir, Specialist, Metropolitan Police, Reykjavík, 28 November 2016 (two separate meetings).

- Andrés Ragnarsson and Einar Gylfi Jónsson, Therapists, Home Peace – Treatment and Knowledge Centre for Perpetrators, Treatment Programme for Perpetrators, 28 November 2016.

- Halldóra Gunnarsdóttir, Gender Equality Adviser, Human Rights Office, Reykjavik City, United Against Domestic Violence Steering Group, 28 November 2016.

- Stefanía Sörheller, Social Services, United Against Domestic Violence Steering Group, 28 November 2016.

- Anna Kristinsdóttir, Director, Human Rights Office, Reykjavik City, United Against Domestic Violence Steering Group, 28 November 2016.

- Halldóra Dröfn Gunnarsdóttir, Child Protection services in Reykjavík, United Against Domestic Violence Steering Group, 28 November 2016.

- Ástþóra Kristinsdóttir, Health Care System, United Against Domestic Violence Steering Group, 28 November 2016.

- Sigþrúður Guðmundsdóttir, The Women's Shelter, United Against Domestic Violence Steering Group, 28 November 2016.

- Marta Birna Baldursdóttir, Head of Division, Ministry of Finance and Economic Affairs, Department of Public Management and Reform, Iceland, 28 November 2016.

- Ólafur Örn Bragason, Psychologist and Head of NCIP Educational Centre, Margrét Herdís Jónsdóttir, Guðbjörg S. Bergsdóttir and Guðrún Sesselja Baldursdóttir, Office of the National Police Commissioner of the Icelandic Police, 29 November 2016.

- Skúli Jónsson, Superintendent, Suðurnes Police District, *Keeping the Window Open – The Suðurnes Project*, 29 November 2016.

- Guðmundur Sigurðsson, Detective, Suðurnes Police District, *Keeping the Window Open – The Suðurnes Project*, 29 November 2016.

- Súsanna Björg Fróðadóttir, Lawyer, Suðurnes Police District, *Keeping the Window Open – The Suðurnes Project*, 29 November 2016.

- Hera Ósk Einarsdóttir, Director of Welfare, Reykjanesbær municipality, *Keeping the Window Open – The Suðurnes Project*, 29 November 2016.

- Sigríður Björk Guðjónsdóttir, Chief of Reykjavik Metropolitan Police, *Keeping the Window Open – The Suðurnes Project*, 29 November 2016.

- Erica Schriek, advisor, FFP Supervisor and Team Manager Secretaryteams, Jeugdbescherming Regio Amsterdam, 7 December 2016.

- Sigrid van de Poel, Head of Board of Directors, Jeugdbescherming Regio Amsterdam, 7 December 2016.

- Mirjam Coret, Vanguard Advisor and Systems Thinking Consultant, Efexis, 7 December 2016.

- Joris Foekema, Team Manager Facilities, Jeugdbescherming Regio Amsterdam, 8 December 2016.

- Marc Dinkgreve, Ambassador of Knowledge, Jeugdbescherming Regio Amsterdam, 8 December 2016.

- Antonietta Perini, Team Manager Youth Protection Academy, Jeugdbescherming Regio Amsterdam, 8 December 2016.

- Marc Dinkgreve, Ambassador of Knowledge, Jeugdbescherming Regio Amsterdam, 8 December 2016.

- Sirpa Kekkonen, Head of Government Strategy Secretariat, Prime Minister's Office, Finland, and Juha Leppänen, CEO, Demos Helsinki, 30 November 2016.

- Johanna Kotipelto, Senior Specialist Policy Analysis Unit Prime Minister's Office, 30 November 2016.

- Juha Leppänen, CEO; Mikko Annala, Head of Governance Innovation and Jaakko Kuosmanen, Adviser, 1 December 2016.

- Kalle Nieminen, Specialist, Ratkaisu 100-Challenge Prize, SITRA, 1 December 2016.

- Paula Laine, Director, Strategy, SITRA, 1 December 2016.

- Olli-Pekka Heinonen, Director General, Finnish National Board of Education, 1 December 2016.

- Kaisa Lähteenmäki-Smith, Science Specialist, Ira Alanko, Project Manager, and Johanna Kotipelto, Senior Specialist Policy Analysis Unit Prime Minister's Office, 2 December 2016.

- Airja Terho, Ministerial Adviser, Ministry of Finance, Finland, 2 December 2016.

- Seungho Lee, Design for Government Programme, Aalto University, 2 December 2016.

- Marco Steinberg, CEO, Snowcone & Haystack, 2 December 2016.

- Juha Leppänen, CEO; Mikko Annala, Head of Governance Innovation, and Jaakko Kuosmanen, Adviser, 2 December 2016.

- Annukka Berg, Senior Specialist, Government Policy Analysis Unit & Senior Researcher, Finnish Environment Institute 5 January 2017 (teleconference).

- Olli E. Kangas, Head of the Research Department, KELA, 11 January 2017 (Skype).

- Roger Halliday, Chief Statistician and Head of Performance, Scottish Government, 16 March 2017 (teleconference).

- Alisa Cook, Director, Outcome Focus, 29 March 2017 (teleconference).

ORGANISATION FOR ECONOMIC CO-OPERATION AND DEVELOPMENT

The OECD is a unique forum where governments work together to address the economic, social and environmental challenges of globalisation. The OECD is also at the forefront of efforts to understand and to help governments respond to new developments and concerns, such as corporate governance, the information economy and the challenges of an ageing population. The Organisation provides a setting where governments can compare policy experiences, seek answers to common problems, identify good practice and work to co-ordinate domestic and international policies.

The OECD member countries are: Australia, Austria, Belgium, Canada, Chile, the Czech Republic, Denmark, Estonia, Finland, France, Germany, Greece, Hungary, Iceland, Ireland, Israel, Italy, Japan, Korea, Latvia, Luxembourg, Mexico, the Netherlands, New Zealand, Norway, Poland, Portugal, the Slovak Republic, Slovenia, Spain, Sweden, Switzerland, Turkey, the United Kingdom and the United States. The European Union takes part in the work of the OECD.

OECD Publishing disseminates widely the results of the Organisation's statistics gathering and research on economic, social and environmental issues, as well as the conventions, guidelines and standards agreed by its members.

OECD PUBLISHING, 2, rue André-Pascal, 75775 PARIS CEDEX 16
(04 2017 10 1 P) ISBN 978-92-64-27985-8 – 2017

CPSIA information can be obtained
at www.ICGtesting.com
Printed in the USA
FSHW020632130919
61972FS

9 789264 279858